Second Seminole War 1835–42

COMBAT

Seminole Warrior
VERSUS
US Soldier

Ron Field

Illustrated by Adam Hook

OSPREY PUBLISHING
Bloomsbury Publishing Plc
Kemp House, Chawley Park, Cumnor Hill, Oxford OX2 9PH, UK
29 Earlsfort Terrace, Dublin 2, Ireland
1385 Broadway, 5th Floor, New York, NY 10018, USA
E-mail: info@ospreypublishing.com
www.ospreypublishing.com

OSPREY is a trademark of Osprey Publishing Ltd

First published in Great Britain in 2022

A catalog record for this book is available from the British Library.

ISBN: PB 9781472846884; eBook 9781472846891;
ePDF 9781472846860; XML 9781472846877

22 23 24 25 26 10 9 8 7 6 5 4 3 2 1

Maps by www.bounford.com
Index by Rob Munro
Typeset by PDQ Digital Media Solutions, Bungay, UK
Printed and bound in India by Replika Press Private Ltd.

Osprey Publishing supports the Woodland Trust, the UK's leading
woodland conservation charity.

To find out more about our authors and books visit
www.ospreypublishing.com. Here you will find extracts, author
interviews, details of forthcoming events and the option to sign up for
our **newsletter**.

Acknowledgments

The author would like to thank the following: Erin Beasley, Digital
Image Rights & Reproduction Specialist, Smithsonian National Portrait
Gallery, Washington, DC; Kayla Beth, Rights and Contracts Assistant,
Florida University Press; Joanna Bouldin, McClung Historical Collection
Archivist, East Tennessee History Center, Knoxville, Tennessee; Eric
Duncan, Marketing Director, Cowan's Auctions, Cincinnati, OH;
Elizabeth E. Engel, CA, Senior Archivist, Center for Missouri Studies,
The State Historical Society of Missouri, Columbia, MO; the Foster
family; Kieran O. Holland, Senior Registrar, Museum of Florida History,
Florida Department of State; Katie Horstman, Director of American
History, Cowan's Auctions, Cincinnati, OH; John and Mary Lou Missall;
Kay Peterson, Rights & Reproductions, National Museum of American
History, Smithsonian Institution, Washington, DC; Felicia G. Pickering,
Retired Ethnology Museum Specialist, Department of Anthropology,
National Museum of Natural History, Smithsonian Museum Support
Center, Washington, DC; Jennifer Potts, Curator of Objects, Delaware
Historical Society, Wilmington, DE; Rebecca Hoback P'Simer, Curator
of Collections, East Tennessee Historical Society, Knoxville, Tennessee;
and Steve Rinck.

Author's note

Modern spellings of place names and other geographical locations have
been used in the maps.

Artist's note

Readers may care to note that the original paintings from which the
color plates in this book were prepared are available for private sale. All
reproduction copyright whatsoever is retained by the publishers. All
inquiries should be addressed to:

scorpiopaintings@btinternet.com

The publishers regret that they can enter into no correspondence upon
this matter.

CONTENTS

Introduction

Wading through thick black swamp water, the US regulars and volunteers commanded by Major General Thomas S. Jesup struggled over slippery cypress roots as they approached the dense hammock (a stand of trees on elevated land surrounded by wetland) of southern live oak occupied by Seminole warriors near the Loxahatchee River, in Southern Florida, on January 24, 1838. Suddenly they were met by a flash of rifle fire and blood-curdling war-whoops from the depths of the undergrowth facing them. At the same time, US artillery opened fire, belching flame and smoke as the projectiles arced over the advancing troops. Attached to Jesup's staff, Assistant Surgeon Jacob Rhett Motte wrote later that the guns

> … did effective service by throwing grape and shells into the thickest of the bushes. Congreve rockets also contributed their terrible whizzing toward increasing and stunning uproar that raged on all sides. The Indians yelled and shrieked; the rifles cracked, and their balls whistled; the musketry rattled; the congreve [*sic*] rockets whizzed; the artillery bellowed; the shells burst; and take it all in all there was created no small racket for awhile. (Sunderman 1953: 194)

In the last pitched battle of the Second Seminole War (1835–42), the warriors under Chiefs Halleck-Hajo and Tuskegee fought stubbornly in defense of a homeland that most of them were ultimately destined to lose.

The name "Seminole" derives from the Creek word *simanooli* meaning "runaway," reflecting the fact that the Seminoles were descendants of various Lower Creek tribes from Georgia who migrated into Spanish Florida in the late 18th century. Later the Lower Creeks were joined by larger numbers of Upper Creeks from Alabama, but the two peoples spoke separate languages. Mixing with remnants of the destroyed Apalachee people of northern Florida, plus numerous escaped African slaves, they formed the Seminole confederation, and were considered one of the "Five Civilized Tribes." By the early 19th century,

OPPOSITE
Published in 1896 in Kirk Munroe's *Through Swamp and Glade: A Tale of the Seminole War*, this lithograph by French artist Victor S. Pérard depicts Seminole warriors defending a hammock as US troops advance through swamp water toward them. (Internet Archive)

Consolidating his military success in the First Seminole War in 1818–19, and political successes as Territorial Governor of Florida in 1821 and President of the United States from 1829 through 1837, Andrew Jackson ruthlessly pursued his policy involving the removal of Native Americans, including the Seminoles, to Indian Territory west of the Mississippi River. (Courtesy National Gallery of Art, Washington, D.C., Andrew W. Mellon Collection, 1942.8.34)

the Seminole confederation had adopted many of the aspects of white frontier society and treated many runaway Blacks as slaves, lived in cabins, raised crops, herded cattle, and traded with the United States, Britain, and Spain.

American encroachment into Spanish Florida began on July 27, 1816 when a punitive expedition led by Major General (Brevet) Edmund P. Gaines destroyed an earthen redoubt on the Apalachicola River occupied by Seminoles and escaped African-American slaves known as the "Negro Fort." This was followed two years later by an invasion led by Major General Andrew Jackson, which began the First Seminole War (1818–19) and resulted in the Spanish capitulation of posts at St. Marks and Pensacola, and a US victory against the Seminoles and their African-American allies at Suwanee.

Following the signing of the Adams–Onís Treaty on February 22, 1819, which marked the cession of Florida to the United States by Spain, its ratification by both countries during 1820, and the implementation of its terms on February 22, 1821, Andrew Jackson, having resigned his commission in the US Army, served as the first Territorial Governor of Florida from July 17 to December 1, 1821. Large numbers of American settlers began colonizing northern Florida during the next decade, but as conflicts occurred more frequently with the settlers, the Seminoles were driven away from the more favorable west coast of Florida and into the extensive wetlands of the interior. As a result of the Treaty of Moultrie Creek, signed on September 18, 1823, the Seminoles were forced to relinquish to the United States all claims to land in Florida and were required to move onto a reservation in the central part of the territory.

Although promises were made to provide financial aid and support to Seminole farmers on reservation land, the Federal government failed to honor the terms of the treaty, which led to famine and increased resentment toward white encroachment. To make matters worse, a flood in 1826 resulted in further starvation among the Seminoles. In 1826, Governor William P. Duval of Florida conducted a tour of the land granted to the Seminoles, and observed: "The best of the Indian lands are worth but little; nineteen-twentieths of their whole country, with the present boundary, is by far the poorest and most miserable region I ever beheld" (*American State Papers* "Indian Affairs," Vol. 2: 664).

The election of Andrew Jackson as the seventh president of the United States on December 2, 1828 had a further profound effect on American–Indian relations in Florida, and reflected Jackson's Indian fighter past and lack of regard for the Native American. The Indian Removal Act passed on May 26, 1830 authorized Jackson to negotiate treaties to buy tribal lands in the east in exchange for lands to be known as Indian Territory west of the Mississippi River and outside the existing state borders of the United States.

On May 9, 1832, the principal Seminole chiefs were induced to sign the Treaty of Payne's Landing, which provided that a delegation of tribal representatives should visit the Indian Territory and report on its suitability as a new home. While out west, the delegation was persuaded by Indian Agent Wiley Thompson to sign the Treaty of Fort Gibson on March 28, 1833, by which they agreed to the removal of the whole Seminole nation from Florida. However, upon the return of the delegation to Florida, disagreements broke out, with some chiefs denying that they had signed the treaty. Others claimed they had been forced into signing. All the chiefs agreed that they had been sent strictly as advisors, and that the final decision should be made by the Seminole tribal council.

Despite much opposition, both treaties were ratified during April 1834, and the deadline for the final removal of the Seminoles from Florida, to be supervised by Thompson, was set for January 1, 1836. Meanwhile, Brevet Brigadier General Duncan L. Clinch was ordered to take command of the regular troops in the territory in preparation for the removal operation.

At a meeting with Seminole leaders on April 24, 1835, Thompson informed Chief Micanopy, or Crazy Alligator, that he should prepare his people to embark at an early date on steamers at Tampa Bay. Attending the talks as an interpreter for the Seminole chief was Abraham, a Black ex-slave. When a final ultimatum to leave Florida was put to Micanopy, Abraham responded, "The old man says to-day the same he said yesterday, 'that the nation had decided in council to decline the offer of the United States Government'" (quoted in McCall 1868: 302).

Tensions between the Seminoles and the whites continued to heighten during the remainder of 1835 as the Native Americans prepared to fight, while gathering in what crops they could and removing their families to the interior of the territory. Meanwhile, many more Floridian settlers enlisted in the militia and landowners began fortifying their plantations and farms. Although Thompson attempted to befriend Chief Osceola, or The Black Drink, and also known as Billy Powell, and even gifted him a rifle, the Seminole chief continued to resist any talk of removal plans. Frequently visiting Fort King, Osceola on one occasion confronted Thompson so fiercely he was clapped in irons for two days until he agreed to be more respectful. In order to secure his release, Osceola promised to sign both the treaties, but secretly prepared vengeance against Thompson.

Further incidents added to the tension. On June 19, 1835 a skirmish occurred near the Hog's Town Settlement when a Seminole hunting party left the reservation and was accosted by some white settlers who fatally wounded one Indian. Seeking revenge, on August 11 the Seminoles shot dead and scalped Private Kinsley H. Dalton, Co. H, 3d Artillery, near Hillsborough

The most extreme reaction to the Treaty of Fort Gibson came from Osceola, who was an advisor to Micanopy, the principal chief of the Seminoles. When confronted with the treaty document by Indian Agent Wiley Thompson, Osceola stated, "The land is ours; we do not need an agent," following which he is reputed to have drawn a knife and thrust it through the paper and into the table adding, "This is the only way I will sign" (Coe 1898: 51). Evidence suggesting that this event occurred is supported by a small triangular hole shaped like the point of a knife in the center of the treaty document, now preserved in the US National Archives. This lithograph print by R.J. Hamerton was published in 1841 in *A Narrative of the Early Days and Remembrances of Oceola Nikkanochee*, written by Andrew Welch. (Internet Archive)

The battles explored in this book took place in the United States territory of Florida. Following the refusal of the Seminoles to be removed to Indian Territory west of the Mississippi River, a small military column led by Brevet Major Francis L. Dade, 4th Infantry, was massacred by a Seminole force led by Chief Micanopy as they marched to the relief of Fort King on December 28, 1835. With the escalation of hostilities following the Dade Massacre, US troops conducted several unsuccessful campaigns against the Seminoles during 1836. By 1837 the main efforts of the US Army were concentrated on driving the Seminole people south of a line running from Smyrna on the east (Atlantic) coast to Fort Brooke on the west (Gulf) coast. As a result, the Seminoles were forced into the swamplands of Southern Florida. This US strategy was consolidated during the course of 1837 with the military campaign of Colonel Zachary Taylor, which resulted in a closely contested action with Seminoles led by Chief Abiaka, or Sam Jones, at the battle of Lake Okeechobee on December 25, 1837. The last large-scale pitched battle of the Second Seminole War took place at the Loxahatchee River, or Turtle River, on January 24, 1838, where troops under Major General Thomas S. Jesup overcame a smaller Seminole force, led by Chiefs Halleck-Hajo and Tuskegee, which was forced to retreat in the face of much greater US firepower. During the remaining four years of the war, US forces consolidated their control throughout Florida by constructing numerous forts to police the territory, while conducting small-scale US Army/Navy operations to round up most of the remaining Seminole people and transport them to Indian Territory.

Bridge as he carried mail along the King Highway military road between Fort Brooke and Fort King.

Civil war broke out among the Seminoles in late November 1835. Outraged by the actions of those who had agreed to removal, Osceola determined to kill their leader Charley Emathla. On November 26 Osceola led a party of about 400 warriors to Emathla's village and shot him dead as he returned home from selling his cattle (Porter 1946: 19).

What might be considered the first serious action of the Second Seminole War occurred at Payne's Prairie on December 18, 1835 when about 60 Seminoles attacked a military wagon train belonging to a scouting expedition of Florida mounted militia led by Colonel John Warren – having killed three men and wounded five, the Seminoles stripped the wagons of valuable ammunition and supplies. The next day another column of Florida militia commanded by Major William Wyatt arrived at the scene of the attack and shortly after encountered a party of Seminoles. According to Wyatt,

> The Indians took [to] a thick scrub surrounding a small grassy pond, where they were in a short time surrounded by our troops; we killed all the Indians that were thus surrounded, 4 of which we saved, and others no doubt, were left dead in the water … Our Middle Florida Volunteers charged the scrub with a firmness unparalleled in the history of Indian Warfare. (*CDC*, January 5, 1836: 2:2)

On December 23, 1835, a column of US regulars under Brevet Major Francis L. Dade, 4th Infantry, set out from Fort Brooke on the 100-mile march to reinforce the garrison at Fort King and carry out the final removal of the Seminoles by force if necessary. Three days later, with the deadline for their removal looming, the Seminole chiefs decided to take decisive action to defend their right to remain in Florida. Of their plan of attack, Chief Halpatter-Tustenuggee, or Alligator, recalled: "We had been preparing for this more than a year. Though promises had been made to assemble on the 1st of January [1836]. It was not to leave the country, but to fight for it" (quoted in Sprague 1848: 90).

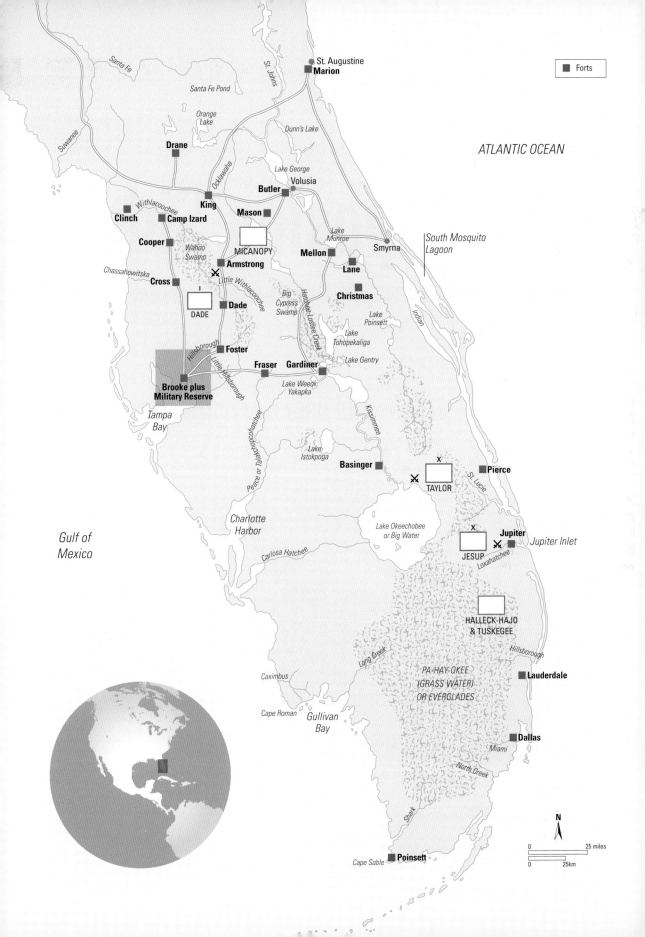

The Opposing Sides

ORIGINS AND ORGANIZATION

Seminole

According to Richard K. Call, the third Governor of the Territory of Florida, the Seminoles and their allies could field between 1,200 and 2,000 warriors of either Indian or African-American origin at the beginning of the Second

A nephew of Seminole Chief Micanopy, Coacoochee was captured with Osceola on October 21, 1837, under a white flag of truce and imprisoned in Fort Marion, St. Augustine, but escaped on the night of November 29/30 and fought at Lake Okeechobee on December 25. He was eventually captured on June 4, 1841 and on October 11 that year was sent to the Indian reservation in Arkansas Territory. This illustration was published in 1848 in John T. Sprague's *The Origin, Progress, and Conclusion of the Florida War.* (Internet Archive)

Seminole War. These were supplemented by an unknown number of Creeks (*American State Papers* "Military Affairs," Vol. 7: 218). The numbers dwindled considerably during the course of the war as chiefs, subtribes, and clans surrendered or reluctantly turned themselves in for migration west.

Much of the organization, training, and customs of the Seminoles were based on Creek culture, social order, and warfare. They formed themselves into clans, which tended to live in their own *talwas* or towns. At the top of the

Seminole warrior

This plate depicts a Seminole warrior about to fire on the column led by Brevet Major Francis L. Dade following the first signal shot fired by Chief Micanopy. Approximately half the column of US troops fell dead or wounded as a result of this first volley.

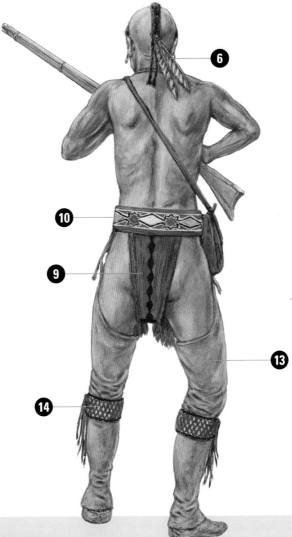

Weapons, dress, and equipment

His main weapon is a "Wickham Type" Indian Trade Rifle (**1**), which was a smoothbore version of the Model 1814 Common Rifle. This weapon has been altered from flintlock to percussion and fires a .54-caliber ball; it has iron mounts and an oval patch box in the butt. Its maximum range was about 300yd with an effective range of only about 50yd or less. Attached to the warrior's waist belt is a spear-pointed knife (**2**) in a leather sheaf decorated with painted and dyed porcupine quills. The knife handle is incised with an irregular pattern. His cartridges and caps are carried in a leather pouch (**3**) worn over his left shoulder with the pouch on the right hip.

His hair (**4**) is cut close to the head, except for a strip about 1in wide running over the front of the scalp from temple to temple, and another strip, of about the same width, perpendicular to the former, crossing the crown of the head to the nape of the neck. At each temple a heavy tuft of hair (**5**) is allowed to hang to the bottom of the lobe of the ear. The long hair of the strip crossing to the neck is

gathered and braided into two ornamental queues. He has two wild turkey feathers tied into his hair (**6**), and his face is painted with half-circles beneath his eyes, and large circles on each cheek (**7**), the colors representing war and death respectively. He also wears a moustache and imperial or goatee beard on his face. His chest and arms are also streaked with paint (**8**).

Clothing includes a cotton breech cloth (**9**) with appliquéd edging, and tassels. Fastened around his waist with tassels is a narrow leather belt (**10**) with a wool cloth panel inset with glass beadwork. A gorget (**11**) of plain hammered silver and a star-pattern medallion (**12**) are hung around his neck. Supported by leather thongs tied around his waist belt, his buckskin leggings (**13**) are made of deerskin. Leg garters (**14**) made of finger-woven wool yarn, with miniature glass beads, are tied just below his knees. His plain moccasins (**15**) are each made from one piece of buckskin gathered together and stitched in a pucker on top of the foot and behind the heel.

social hierarchy, the town elders were responsible for electing the *talwa* leader known as the *Mico*, the chief of the clan (Covington 1993: 6). The Seminoles generally adhered to the Creek traditions of warfare and placed their warriors into four classes, which were selected by the clan elders. The *tustunugee* was regarded as a war leader, the *imala lakalgi* and the *labotskalgi* were of secondary and tertiary importance, and the *Imala* was the lowest class of warrior.

Having earned his position based upon his prowess in combat, the *tustunugee* was charged with mustering the warriors and leading them during raids. In the event of war, he gathered the warriors by placing a red club in the town square. He also placed a number of red sticks, to signify the number of days before the warriors must gather, in the hands of war leaders from neighboring bands and directed them to muster their warriors. Once gathered, the warriors sat in the council lodge to listen to the war plans of the *tustunugee* and make final preparations for the impending action (Covington 1993: 7).

Once a *tustunugee* had secured followers for his war party, tradition required that the party perform certain rituals. Every warrior set out to purify himself in order to suppress the wants of the flesh by taking part with others in the ceremony of the black drink, which was a strong emetic that thoroughly cleansed the digestive tract. Seated in a circle, the warriors received the potion from a medicine man and swallowed it in heavy drafts, following which each warrior would experience stomach pains and projectile vomit for some time until his system was empty. Following this, the warriors fasted and refrained from cohabiting with their women. Thus, purity and abstention would lead them to victory. Even on the expedition which followed, however, the warriors ate little and took little rest. Vestiges of these ancient practices still existed in 1836; but the nature of the Second Seminole War, which involved guerrilla tactics involving smaller numbers rather than larger war parties going into battle, meant these practices and rituals faded out and warriors ate and drank whenever they could. Some imbibed alcohol when it could be procured (Mahon 2017: 14).

US Army

On the eve of the Second Seminole War, the aggregate strength of the US Army was 7,151 officers and men composed of the 1st through 7th Infantry, 1st through 4th Artillery, and the Regiment of Dragoons (*American State Papers* "Military Affairs," Vol. 5: 634). The regiments were scattered throughout the United States for the defense of the inland and maritime frontiers, with only nine companies of artillery and two companies of infantry – altogether only 26 officers and 510 men – posted in Florida (Risch 1989: 220).

As a result of the demand for a greater force of the regular army to overcome the Seminoles, elements of the 2d, 3d, and 4th Artillery, and 2d Dragoons, plus a battalion of US Marines, were also required to serve as infantry in the swamplands of Florida. By November 30, 1836, a total of 76 officers and 1,681 men of all branches of service were posted in the territory. By November 30, 1837, the regular force had increased to 230 officers and 4,322 men and, although numbers were reduced as the Seminoles were subjugated during the next three years, there were still 186 officers and 3,615 men on duty in Florida in 1841. This regular force was supplemented throughout most of the war by Floridian mounted volunteers, plus those from states such as Tennessee, Alabama, and Louisiana. Enlisted for terms of three, six, or 12 months, all these volunteers were also often required to fight on foot (Sprague 1848: 103–06).

From 1821 through 1836, the company was at its smallest size in the US Army. The infantry company had a maximum authorized strength of three officers consisting of one captain, one first lieutenant, and one second lieutenant, and 51 enlisted men composed of three sergeants, four corporals, two musicians, and 42 private soldiers. An artillery company had the same number of privates, but its aggregate was larger because of two additional

OPPOSITE

Seminole Chief Ee-mat-lá, or King Phillip, was painted by George Catlin while imprisoned at Fort Moultrie, near Charleston, South Carolina, in January 1838. Catlin described him as a "very aged chief, who has been a man of great notoriety and distinction in his time" (Catlin 1845: 220). Ee-mat-lá died on October 8, 1839, while being transported west (Catlin, *Letters and Notes*, vol. 2, no. 57, 1841; reprint 1973). (Smithsonian American Art Museum, Gift of Mrs. Joseph Harrison, Jr., 1985.66.302)

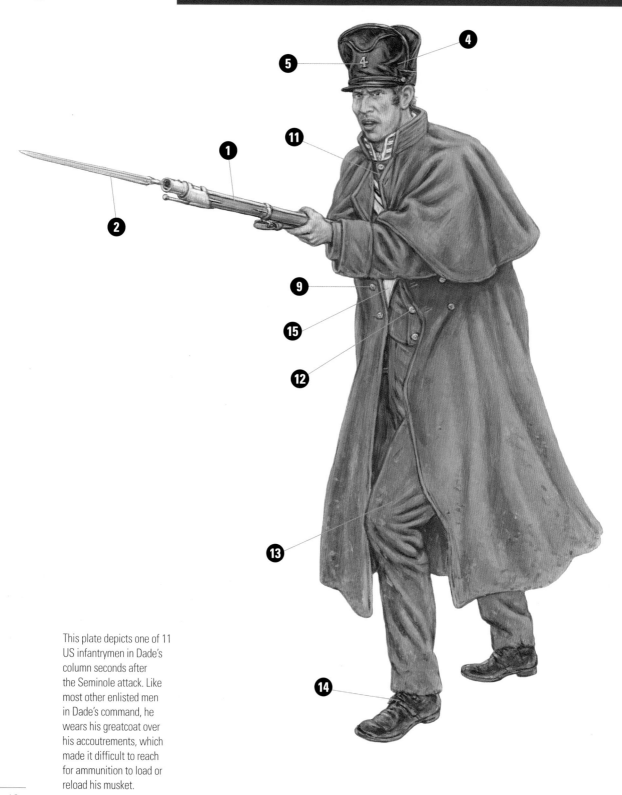

This plate depicts one of 11 US infantrymen in Dade's column seconds after the Seminole attack. Like most other enlisted men in Dade's command, he wears his greatcoat over his accoutrements, which made it difficult to reach for ammunition to load or reload his musket.

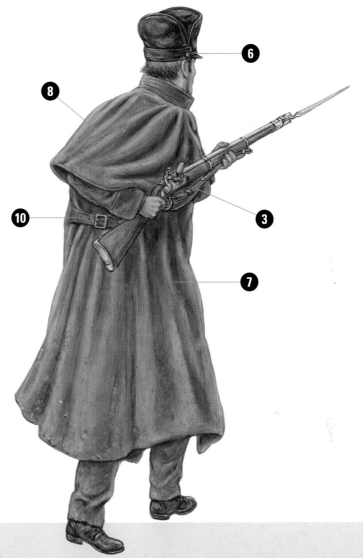

Weapons, dress, and equipment

He is armed with a Model 1816 smoothbore flintlock musket (**1**); it fired a .69-caliber musket ball and had a rate of fire of two to three rounds a minute in well-trained hands. Attached are a socket bayonet (**2**) and a russet leather sling (**3**).

His headgear (**4**) consists of a Pattern 1833 folding leather forage cap with brass regimental number "4" at the front (**5**) and "eagle"-pattern button holding the chin strap in place (**6**). Unbuttoned in order to reach his cartridge box, his double-breasted infantry-pattern wool greatcoat (**7**) has a stand-up collar, elbow-length cape (**8**), and pressed white metal buttons (**9**). A short belt and buckle (**10**) at the rear adjusts the waist. Underneath this he wears a Pattern 1832 twilled cotton cloth jacket (**11**) with white trim on the collar and shoulder straps, fastened with a single row of nine white metal "eagle I" buttons (**12**). Trousers (**13**) consist of close-fitting, plain woolen "overalls." On his feet are "straight last" (neither left nor right foot) leather lace-up bootees (**14**).

Obscured under his greatcoat, accoutrements consist of a 2¼in-wide Pattern 1828 buff leather cross-belt (**15**) worn over his left shoulder, with pick and brush set attached, supporting a Pattern 1828 black leather cartridge box on his right hip. The box contains a wooden block bored for 26 cartridges and a three-sectioned tin underneath the block for an additional 12 cartridges and cleaning rags. Each man in Dade's command carried only 30 rounds of ammunition. Worn over his right shoulder is another Pattern 1828 white buff-leather belt, with a Pattern 1826 round "eagle" breast plate attached, supporting a Pattern 1828 bayonet scabbard holding a Pattern 1816 bayonet on his left hip. Worn under his greatcoat from his right shoulder is a white cotton haversack, with a strap of the same material, fastened by three small metal buttons, plus a metal-banded, wooden cheesebox-pattern canteen painted Prussian blue and decorated with white letters "U.S." plus regimental number "4" and company letter "B."

lieutenants, one extra sergeant, and three artificers. As for the regiment, those in the infantry branch of service had ten companies while those in the artillery had nine. Owing to the need for a greater military presence in Florida, artillery regiments were increased in size during 1838 with the addition of Co. K, while the number of private soldiers in artillery companies was temporarily increased by 16, bringing the number up to 58. Infantry companies were enlarged with the addition of a sergeant and 38 privates. At the same time the number of second lieutenants in infantry companies was reduced to one.

The effective strength of a military unit seldom equaled its authorized strength due to lack of recruits, detailed duty, sickness, and absences. For example, while stationed at Key West, Florida, in 1835, Co. B, 4th Infantry, had only two officers, three noncommissioned officers, one musician, and 37 privates. On January 12, 1838, Colonel Zachary Taylor wrote that there was a great deficiency of officers among the ranks of the regulars, as well as the rank and file of the companies, particularly in the 1st Infantry which was under 50 per cent its manpower, and averaged 23 men per company. (Kersey & Peterson 1997: 452–53).

Recruiting rendezvous points for the US Army were established in many cities, and recruiting parties consisted of one commissioned officer, one NCO, and two privates. Recruits enlisted for three years and had to be between the ages of 18 and 35, and above 5ft 6in tall. Those recruits under age 21 had to provide written permission from their parents. At the beginning of the war, monthly pay for an infantry sergeant major, quartermaster sergeant, chief musician, and chief bugler was $16; first sergeants received, $15; all other sergeants, $12; corporals, $8; buglers and musicians, $6; and privates, $6 (*NS*, September 16, 1836: 4:4).

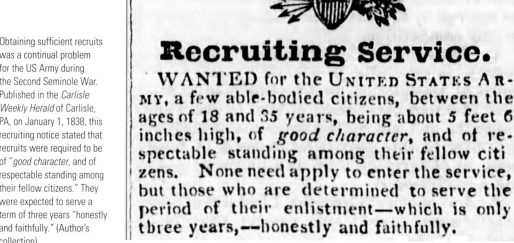

Obtaining sufficient recruits was a continual problem for the US Army during the Second Seminole War. Published in the *Carlisle Weekly Herald* of Carlisle, PA, on January 1, 1838, this recruiting notice stated that recruits were required to be of "*good character*, and of respectable standing among their fellow citizens." They were expected to serve a term of three years "honestly and faithfully." (Author's collection)

A runaway slave who had served as an interpreter for Micanopy since 1825, Abraham is pictured in this wood engraving by Nathaniel Orr (1822–1908) wearing a typical Seminole turban and fringed hunting shirt. Also known as "The Prophet," he assured the Seminoles that "God was in their favor," and prophesied that Wiley Thompson would be "killed by Indians while walking about his place" (*ANC*, November 3, 1836: 285). His prophecy was realized on December 28, 1835. When the war began Abraham was one of the leading "war spirits," and personally commanded 80 warriors. This illustration was published in 1848 in John T. Sprague's *The Origin, Progress, and Conclusion of the Florida War*. (Internet Archive)

TRAINING AND TACTICS

Seminole

The Seminoles engaged in three forms of combat during the course of the Second Seminole War. For the first two years they fought both large- and small-scale battles, as well as carrying out attacks on forts and blockhouses. Following the battle of Loxahatchee River on January 24, 1838, and in response to US tactics, they changed from fighting large-scale battles to moving in smaller, decentralized forces to conduct small-scale, guerrilla-style attacks. It is likely that strategies such as this had been used in the past by the Creek peoples as well as other Muskhogean groups throughout the southeast (West & Belko 2011: 155).

As masters of guerrilla warfare, the Seminoles maneuvered in flexible formations, attacked, and disappeared, and used the Florida terrain as a weapon against their enemy. In his analysis of the war, David S.B. Butler explains how they used the terrain to best advantage. He defined the woodland fortress and described how hammocks served the Seminoles as a form of natural fortification while its discrete borders served as the outline of an impromptu stockade (Butler 2001: 50). Additionally, the swamps and rivers served as moats and as avenues of escape and natural barriers to hinder the advance of the US soldiers.

A Seminole raiding party would advance on its objective in a single file, each warrior following carefully in the footsteps of the other, while the very last warrior concealed the raiding party's tracks by brushing them away with a tree branch. During such maneuvers, the warriors adhered to strict discipline. Orders were communicated via hand signals and only the *tustunugee* could order a halt, at which point the warriors quickly formed a circle with their firearms at the ready. The Seminole warriors also executed this formation every time they halted for rest or sleep (Covington 1993: 7).

When involved in larger-scale actions it was customary for Seminole prophets and visionaries to perform singing and dancing rituals to inspire the warriors and ready them for battle. At the battle of Lake Okeechobee on December 23, 1837 the shaman Otolke-Thlocko, or Big Wind, and also known as "The Prophet," did much to make the warriors feel impervious to enemy musket fire.

US Army

Following enlistment, recruits were transported to military depots in New York City or Newport, Kentucky, where they were trained and drilled for two months before being allocated to a regiment. Drill instruction was based on the three-volume *Infantry-Tactics; or, Rules for the Exercise and Manoeuvres of the United States' Infantry* compiled by Major General Winfield Scott, and adopted by the government for the US Army in 1835. Volume II of this work contained "Instruction for Light Infantry and Rifle, or Skirmishers," which was particularly applicable to conditions in Florida. A notable exception to this was the 4th Infantry, commanded by Lieutenant Colonel William S. Foster, which continued until 1838 to employ Scott's light-infantry drill published in 1825 as *Infantry Tactics; or, Rules for the Exercise and Manoeuvres of the Infantry of the U.S. Army*. This contained "a compendious system of evolutions for Light Infantry and Riflemen." Before re-deployment to Florida with Co. A, 4th Infantry, Foster wrote Jesup on October 3, 1837 that the 50-strong Co. A, 4th Infantry, he recruited was organized, armed, equipped and drilled in Scott's earlier system (Missall 2005: 117). Foster also trained men under his command to utilize shock tactics when in battle with Seminoles, and on November 13, 1837 wrote his wife that the men were to trained to charge immediately, thereby preventing the enemy from reloading their weapons (Missall 2005: 118).

Serving as a medical aide, Private John Bemrose, 2d Artillery, commented that he had observed soldiers train at Fort King using woodland drill, enabling them to fight like the Seminoles (Bemrose 1966: 25). One of two survivors of the massacre of Dade's column on December 28, 1835, Private Ransom Clark, detached from Co. B, 3d Artillery to serve with Co. C, 2d Artillery, later recalled that when the Seminoles began their second attack, the remaining men were ordered to "form themselves as Light Infantry, each taking a tree" (quoted in Cohen 1836: 70). Light-infantry tactics would later largely supplant close-order formation during the course of the war. Combined with "search and destroy" introduced by Brevet Brigadier General Walker K. Armistead in 1840, the tactics wore the Seminoles down, resulting in the termination of hostilities in August 1842.

Used to defending their frontier communities and homes from Indian attack, the volunteers were more familiar with skirmishing. Volunteers

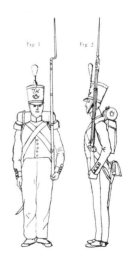

Illustrated in the "School of the Soldier, Part II" of Scott's *Infantry Tactics*, Plate 3 shows the "Principles of Shouldered Arms." A thoroughly drilled infantryman in this position would correctly retain close-order formation, providing an ideal target for Seminole sharpshooters in battle. (Internet Archive)

Published in 1845 in Harry Hazel's *The West Point Cadet; or the Officer's Bride*, this fanciful engraving shows US artillerymen in action at Withlacoochee River wearing full-dress uniforms. More realistically, the Seminoles are depicted concealed in a hammock awaiting an attack. (Library of Congress 6811000)

from states such as Missouri, Tennessee, and Alabama accompanying the regulars did not acquit themselves quite so well in the face of the fearsome Seminoles, however. For this reason they were disliked by regular Army officers, particularly Taylor. Although they were largely lacking drill and training compared to regulars, the volunteers' fighting ability was put to the ultimate test at both Lake Okeechobee and Loxahatchee River where they were ordered forward ahead of well-disciplined infantry and artillery soldiers, which resulted in devastating casualties.

Although they had gained some experience during the First Seminole War, the US generals who fought the Seminoles in the Second Seminole War derived much of their combat knowledge from their successes against the British in the War of 1812 (1812–15). As a result, drill and training was steeped in the traditions of conventional European battlefield tactics. The guerrilla-style warfare of the Seminoles in the humid subtropical climate of Florida was a relatively new experience for the US Army, however. Although they had fought other Native American peoples who refused to engage in orthodox battle, preferring instead lightning-quick ambushes and raids, they had seldom fought an enemy that attacked and then disappeared into a thick undergrowth of hammocks and swampland. In fact, the terrain of Florida posed a considerable hardship for US soldiers who suffered tremendous losses to the tropical heat and a host of diseases that accounted for two-thirds of all US casualties in the war.

The close-order battle formation in which most of the US regular troops and volunteers were required to maneuver and fight at Lake Okeechobee and Loxahatchee River led to unnecessarily high casualties. Nevertheless, morale and discipline among the regular troops remained very high due to a cadre of West Point-trained officers at their head. For example, when Lieutenant Colonel Alexander R. Thompson was mortally wounded while leading the 6th Infantry into battle at Lake Okeechobee his last words were "Keep steady men, charge the hammock – remember the regiment to which you belong!" (*ANC*, February 8, 1838: 84).

APPEARANCE, WEAPONS, AND EQUIPMENT

Seminole

Because their migration into north Florida was the result of the European encroachment, the tribes which became the Seminoles in the 19th century had already replaced most of their traditional apparel with clothing they made from European trade goods. This clothing often copied European patterns.

In peacetime the Seminole warrior was elaborately attired. Posted at Fort Lauderdale in 1838, Assistant Surgeon Ellis Hughes described Tomoka John, who was captured with Chief King Phillip at Dunlawton Plantation during September 1837, as wearing

> dark snuff trousers with dragoon doublings under his legs … White frock coat …
> with a plaid collar over the shoulders à la Highland … moccasins – red leg[ging]s
> – blue beads ornamenting them. Frock tied around body, blue band round waist
> with tassels in front … the frock coat fringed with red calico – various calico collars
> – covered all with tin semi-circle necklace – silver band round his hat's middle – tin
> armlets or bracelets. (Hughes Diary, vol. 2: 18)

In battle the appearance of some Seminole warriors was very different, however. With the exception of their weapons and provisions, they chose to fight virtually naked except for a breech cloth and preferred to carry their ammunition in their mouths, enabling them to load their rifles faster than the enemy. They also believed that wounds could become infected if musket shot and fabric tore into their flesh, thus their lack of clothing and equipment originally served a very practical purpose (Covington 1993: 7). This changed during the course of the Second Seminole War, however, as larger-scale battle action and constant winter campaigning necessitated more clothing be worn for practical purposes. Some warriors wore captured US Army clothing, possibly stripped off the dead after the massacre of Dade's column. During an attack on Camp Izard in March 1836, Brevet 2d Lieutenant Henry Prince, Co. B, 4th Infantry, observed Seminoles "dressed like regular soldiers, some having blue great coats, some even the forage cap – many having short blue jackets and trowsers" (Prince Diary, March 3, 1836).

Regarding warpaint, the Seminole warriors painted their faces and streaked their bodies. In council of war they sometimes applied a half-circle of red paint under each eye. In battle, yellow paint indicated a warrior was ready to die. Red paint signified blood. Green paint under the eyes was meant to improve night vision. A few warriors also had their ears elongated and slit (Mahon 1960: 123).

According to Dr. Frederick Weedon, who attended the ailing warriors Uchee Billy and Osceola after their capture on September 10 and October 21, 1837 respectively, the former asked for some red paint and a looking glass and painted half of his face, his neck, wrists, and backs of his hands, plus the handle of his knife, as a symbol that an irrevocable oath of war and destruction had been sworn (Walkiewicz 2008: 110).

Although the traditional weapons of the Seminole were the bow and arrow, tomahawk, and club, by the beginning of the 19th century they were adept

Based on personal observations while serving at Fort Lauderdale, Assistant Surgeon Ellis Hughes produced these drawings of headgear worn by Seminole warriors in his diary. A simple turban is shown above, while the more elaborate version below is topped with a feather plume. (Ellis Hughes Diary, University of South Florida, Cat. No. H38-00002)

OPPOSITE

Known to the whites as John Hicks, Tuko-See-Mathla or Mole Leader was a Miccosukee Seminole chief. Describing him in his diary, 2d Lieutenant George A. McCall, 1st Infantry wrote, "His frock or coat was of the finest quality and advanced with a quantity of silver ornaments around his neck, arm and wrists, with a gorgeous head-dress of colored shawls. He wore hide moccasins and wool leggings with woven quarters and a bandolier. His bearing was that of a chief indeed" (McCall, 1868: 156). A supporter of the US plan to move the Seminoles across the Mississippi River to Indian Territory in 1835, Tuko-See-Mathla was killed by Osceola, who shot him 16 times. (National Portrait Gallery, Smithsonian Institution; NPG.99.169.6. Gift of Betty A. and Lloyd G. Schermer)

at using firearms for both hunting and warfare. A young warrior captured prior to the battle at Lake Okeechobee was described as being armed with "an excellent rifle, fifty balls in his pouch, and an adequate proportion of powder" (*NNR*, February 10, 1838: 370:2).

Since 1815, the Seminoles had used smoothbore flintlock firearms of a type known as the Indian Rifle, which was a modified version of the .54-caliber Model 1814 Common Rifle designed by Robert T. Wickham and manufactured by Robert Johnson and Henry Deringer, of single-shot pistol fame. The Indian Rifle lacked the rifling in the barrel as the US Government sought to sell Native Americans rifle-like firearms that lacked rifling in order to maintain a tactical advantage, as smoothbore weapons were less accurate than rifled firearms. By the 1830s many of these firearms had been converted to percussion and fired a .54-caliber ball.

By custom Seminoles carried a bandolier bag, while some warriors equipped themselves with leather shot pouches or captured US Army cartridge boxes and belts to accommodate US weapons. The accoutrements of a dead Seminole were described by Prince as consisting of a "powder horn of the very best rifle powder, leather haversack containing large quantity of bullets, pick brush and chain belonging to a musket, flints and other little things" (Prince Diary, March 1, 1836).

US Army

A surgeon accompanying a fresh US infantry detachment as it marched into Seminole territory through a patch of open pine wood noted the men were wearing white cross-belts over their sky-blue jackets with gleaming black leather caps (Troiani 1998: 114). The Florida terrain quickly took its toll on all martial splendor, however. Describing a regular unit he saw in May 1836, at the end of the first campaign, an officer of Colonel Abbott H. Brisbane's South Carolina Regiment wrote: "Here was a company drawn up, which could now scarcely be distinguished by any uniform, except that of dirt, from the common militia; but … their upright heads, and close touching elbows showed that they were regulars; their blue suits were bemired out of recollection, and their brightened belts were now all tarnished" (quoted in Smith 1836: 286).

Months of campaigning in the watery wilderness of swampland in south Florida reduced the uniform and clothing of both regular and volunteer

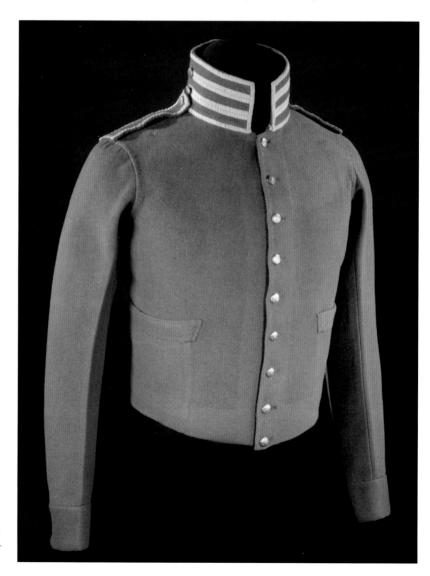

Winter service uniforms for US Army infantry NCOs and enlisted men consisted of a Pattern 1834 sky-blue twilled cotton cloth jacket, or "roundabout," with white branch-of-service trim on the collar and shoulder straps. The front was fastened with a single row of nine white metal "eagle I" buttons. (Division of Political and Military History, National Museum of American History, Smithsonian Institution: 2004-40507: 2004-40507)

soldiery to rags and tatters, particularly with regard to trousers and footwear. A newspaper correspondent accompanying the column commanded by Jesup prior to the battle of Loxahatchee River on January 24, 1838 wrote:

> For nearly two hundred miles, we have passed through an unknown region, cutting roads through dense hammocks, passing innumerable cypress swamps and pine barrens, interspersed with a nearly impassable growth of saw palmetto, and for the last three days wading nearly up to the men's waists in water. Our privations have not been less than our fatigue, the men being nearly naked, and one third of them destitute of shoes. (*ANC*, March 11, 1838: 159)

During the same campaign, an officer of the 2d Dragoons described the troops as "barefooted, their pantaloons cut off as high as the knee by the saw-palmetto …" (quoted in Rodenbough 1875: 31). The foot soldiers of Jesup's command were forced to remain at Fort Jupiter for 11 days after the action at Loxahatchee for want of shoes (*NNR*, September 8, 1839: 15:1).

According to the 1832 Regulations, infantry and artillery officers on winter campaign wore a dark-blue frock coat with plain standing collar and fastened with a single row of ten large regimental buttons, and two small regimental buttons on the cuffs. A crimson silk waist sash was worn under a white leather waist belt fastened with an oval clasp. Trousers were sky-blue with 1½in-wide seam stripe of white for infantry and red for artillery. A white cotton, or linen, shell jacket with a single row of nine small uniform buttons, and two small buttons on cuffs, was worn during the summer months. Dark-blue forage caps were officially worn for all seasons, although brimmed straw hats were preferred by some in extreme summer heat.

Based on the *General Regulations for the Army* published in 1834, winter service uniforms for infantry NCOs and enlisted men consisted of a Pattern 1832 sky-blue twilled cotton cloth jacket with white trim on the collar and shoulder straps, fastened with a single row of nine white metal "eagle I" buttons. Artillery NCOs and enlisted men wore the same pattern of jacket but with yellow trim and "eagle A" buttons.

Some officers preferred to wear the uniform of an enlisted man to avoid being picked off by Seminole sharpshooters. In one of his accounts of Dade's

The Pattern 1833 leather forage cap could be folded flat and had a small flap in the rear that could be lowered into position to protect the neck from the sun and rain. This example was produced by Luke & Wier of New York City, and was worn by 2d Lieutenant Henry Du Pont, 4th Artillery, who was the son of Éleuthère Irénée du Pont, founder of the Du Pont Chemical Company. (From the permanent collection of the Delaware Historical Society)

Massacre, Clark recalled that Captain George W. Gardiner, Co. C, 2d Artillery was "dressed in soldier's clothes" (*CC*, April 20, 1836: 1:1). In his diary, Prince recorded that he carried "a sgts sword old pattern without scabbard" and wore "sergeants [*sic*] pants" (Prince Diary, February 24, 1836).

Noncommissioned officers were denoted by points-up chevrons of white cloth on their sleeves, white being the branch-of-service color for infantry. Artillery enlisted men serving as infantry wore yellow as their branch-of-service color. Trousers consisted of close-fitting sky-blue woolen "overalls," which were plain for all ranks.

During the summer months in Florida, as at all Southern military stations, regular infantrymen wore a lighter-weight white cotton shell jacket and matching overalls, and it is safe to assume that this garb was worn on campaign in the swamps. That worn by officers was described as:

> white cotton or linen, with standing collar; cuffs three and a half inches deep round the wrist, to open at the lower [or rear] seam, where they will be buttoned with two small buttons. A row of ten small uniform buttons down the front at equal distance, the front and rear of the jacket to come down in a peak. (*General Regulations for the Army* 1834: 226)

White cotton drill uniforms were supplied to all three branches of US regular service. The white metal "eagle" buttons and epaulettes on this jacket indicate it was worn by an infantry officer. (Don Troiani)

Double-breasted infantry-pattern greatcoats of blue-gray wool had a stand-up collar and cape which buttoned in front and reached the upper edge of the cuff of the coat. Both flannel and cotton shirts were regular issue, plus canton flannel drawers.

Headgear was the collapsible or folding forage cap of leather, first adopted via General Order No. 38 in 1833, and issued to both officers and men. Describing this cap in a letter to Captain Charles Thurston on April 23, 1833, Commissary General Callender Irvine, head of the Clothing Bureau in Washington, DC, stated that it was "of leather with a patent leather visor … made with one fold at the top; the only ornament … the letter of the Company placed in front" (Clothing Bureau, US National Archives). Because this cap was considered impervious to moisture it did not require a cover, although an accessory for cold climates consisted of a 2½in-wide black fur band that could be "attached to the bottom, to unite in front by a tie of black ribbon" (*General Regulations for the Army* 1834: 228) to add some warmth around the ears and forehead. According to a hospital steward, the infantryman on campaign in Florida wore this while sleeping buckled under the chin to keep insects out of their ears (Troiani 1998: 114).

During the winter of 1838/39, US Army commander Major General Alexander Macomb ordered a new-pattern forage cap. Modeled on a combination of the British Pattern 1825 forage cap and the American civilian hunting and workmen's cap, it had a plain dark-blue cloth top and band, and a leather visor secured with two one-piece "eagle" buttons. Tenders for these caps were advertised in January 1840, and they began to be issued as early as the following September (*NG*, January 1, 1840: 1:3).

Footwear consisted of "straight last" – meaning no left or right – laced bootees, which caused much discomfort. On August 23, 1832, Brevet Lieutenant Colonel Alexander C.W. Fann, 4th Artillery, had complained to Major John Garland in the Clothing Bureau: "On a march, I have frequently seen soldiers take off their shoes, preferring to march barefoot, to suffering pain inflicted by this instrument of torture" (Clothing Bureau, US National Archives).

ABOVE LEFT
This regulation Pattern 1834 waist-belt plate was worn by Lieutenant Colonel William S. Foster, commanding the 4th Infantry at Lake Okeechobee. Produced by Robert Dingee, of New York, only 274 of this pattern were issued to infantry officers. (By permission of the East Tennessee Historical Society)

ABOVE RIGHT
One of a pair of Pattern 1832–51 epaulettes worn by Lieutenant Colonel Foster. The straps and fringe were silver, in line with regulations for infantry. Typical of the Second Seminole War period, a plain metal regimental number "4" is pinned directly onto the strap as opposed to being on a raised embroidered disc. (By permission of the East Tennessee Historical Society)

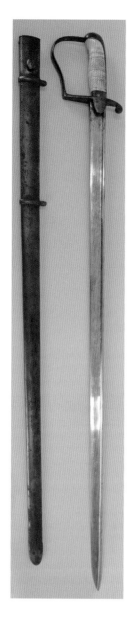

This mounted infantry officer's sword with ivory grip bearing cross-hatched design and "P"-shaped guard, with iron scabbard, was made by Adam W. Spies, of New York City, and was carried by Lieutenant Colonel Foster and probably used during the battle of Lake Okeechobee. (By permission of the East Tennessee Historical Society)

Accoutrements consisted of 2¼in-wide Pattern 1828 white buff-leather cross-belts, Pattern 1808 cartridge boxes with highly ornate Pattern 1832 outer flap (later replaced by a plain flap), and Pattern 1828 bayonet scabbard. Belt plates consisted of a mixture of the oval 1819 brass "US" pattern and round 1826 pattern of white metal, which were unpopular with all ranks. Regarding the cross-belts, an entry in Foster's journal dated February 12, 1836 stated that at night his men lay down with their cartridge boxes and bayonet belts on, but placed under their jackets to hide their white cross belts which provided a perfect target for the enemy (Missall 2005: 20). In order to reduce their conspicuity, blackened cross-belts were issued later in the war, but no other concessions were made to the terrain and climate.

Pattern 1822 cloth knapsacks were painted black and marked in white paint with a bugle suspended by a cord, with the number of the regiment within the cord and the letter of the company below the bugle. The size of this insignia was 6in from the knot of the cord to the curve of the bugle. The numerals and letters were 1½in in height (*General Regulations for the Army* 1834: 232).

Other equipment consisted of a metal-banded wooden canteen painted Prussian blue and decorated with white letters "U.S." and the regimental number and company letter. The canteens were carried on a sling of red-brown or "russet" leather. A white cotton haversack with three buttons was used to carry rations.

Regulation weapons and equipment items were not always carried on campaign in Florida. Following a march through the Big Cypress Swamp, Captain George A. McCall, 4th Infantry, wrote on February 27, 1842: "I carried my seven days' rations in a bag rolled in my blanket and strapped across my shoulders, together with an extra flannel shirt (the only wear on such tramps) and a pair of socks, besides my double gun – swords being worse than useless" (McCall 1868: 398).

The standard firearm for the regular US infantryman was the .69-caliber Model 1816 smoothbore flintlock musket. These firearms were made in the National Armory at Springfield, Massachusetts, and Harpers Ferry, Virginia, or under contract with independent arms-makers. The M1816 musket was a formidable firearm provided with a socket bayonet with a 16in blade and used prepared paper cartridges. Although an infantry musket, it was also issued to artillery units because .69-caliber Model 1817 artillery muskets were in short supply. Leather musket slings were "russet" or red-brown.

About 2.6in in length, the paper cartridges used in muskets during the war were self-contained and included the black-powder charge combined with a lead ball in a paper wrapper used as wadding in the musket barrel. A cotton cord tied round the wrapper separated the projectile from the powder charge, and the wrapper was twisted and folded to close the cartridge base. Cartridges containing a single projectile were termed "ball" cartridges, while those combining a ball with buckshot were known as "buck and ball." Extremely effective and popular with the troops, "buck and ball" contained three buckshot each measuring .34in in diameter, as well as a .69-caliber musket ball. When fired buckshot spread erratically, hitting a number of targets. As a result, rather than fighting in open country the Seminole took every advantage of concealment offered by the dense Florida terrain.

Dade's Massacre

December 28, 1835

Published in 1836 in *An Authentic Narrative of the Seminole War: Its Cause, Rise and Progress*, by Captain James Barr, this hand-colored engraving was intended to serve as propaganda depicting the attacks committed by Seminoles against white settlers in Florida during 1835–36. Shown prominently among those attacking settlers are African Americans, many of whom were escaped slaves, who allied themselves with the Seminoles. (Internet Archive)

BACKGROUND TO BATTLE

When hostilities in the Second Seminole War began in December 1835, the small number of regular US troops in Florida meant settlements and plantations were exposed to possible attacks from the Seminoles. Under overall command of Brevet Brigadier General Clinch whose headquarters were at Fort Drane, which formed part of his "Auld Lang Syne" sugar plantation, these troops were posted at Fort Brooke in Tampa Bay on the west coast, St. Augustine on the east coast, Key West at the southern extremity of the state, and Fort King on the Seminole Reservation in the north-central section of the state. They consisted of nine artillery companies and two infantry companies, a total of only 26 officers and 510 men (Risch 1989: 220).

The above is intended to represent the horrid Massacre of the Whites in Florida, in December 1835, and January, February, March and April 1836, when near Four Hundred (including women and children) fell victims to the barbarity of the Negroes and Indians.

Brevet Brigadier General Duncan L. Clinch commanded the US Army in Florida at the outset of the Second Seminole War and was responsible for the removal of the Seminoles. An experienced soldier who had served in the War of 1812 and First Seminole War, he issued the order for the relief column to march on Fort King, and fought a successful action against the Seminoles at Withlacoochee River on December 31, 1835. He resigned from the US Army on September 21, 1836 and settled into life as a planter near St. Marys, Camden County, Georgia. (Library of Congress: LC-DIG-cwpb-06860)

On December 16, Clinch ordered Captain Gardiner, 2d Artillery, to march a force of two artillery companies serving as infantry from Fort Brooke to the relief of Fort King. This force was to consist of Gardiner's own company, Co. C, 2d Artillery, and Co. B, 3d Artillery, commanded by Captain Upton S. Fraser. As both these companies were under strength, their ranks were supplemented by detachments from Co. B and Co. H, 2d Artillery. On receipt of reports that a strong force of Seminoles had gathered near the forks of the Withlacoochee River, Clinch decided to delay Gardiner's departure until reinforcements were received. Following his arrival from Key West with Co. B, 4th Infantry, Brevet Major Dade, 4th Infantry, offered to command the column as Gardiner's wife was seriously ill, and Gardiner accepted.

Thus reinforced, the column commanded by Dade and composed of eight officers, 99 enlisted men, and three civilians marched out toward Fort King on December 23. The force also included one horse-drawn light supply wagon, and one six-pounder gun supplied with 50 rounds of solid shot and grapeshot, drawn by a team of oxen. The latter caused the column to travel slowly as the oxen quickly became exhausted dragging the gun through the sandy soil and 2d Lieutenant Benjamin Alvord, 4th Infantry, was sent back to Fort Brooke to replace them with a team of horses. Alvord did not rejoin the column (Barr 1836: 9).

Dade was unexpectedly joined by Gardiner, whose wife had been placed on board the schooner *Motto* bound for Key West where their children and her father resided in the barracks. Gardiner was also accompanied by scout and interpreter Luis Fatio Pacheco, a former slave whose loyalty was mistrusted by some of the US military.

Reaching the crossing of the Little Hillsboro River at the end of the first day's march, Dade ordered trees felled and a breastwork erected to protect his camp from attack. According to Chief Halpatter-Tustenuggee, Seminole scouts were watching the progress of the column from "the time the soldiers left the post, and reported each night their place of encampment." Halpatter-Tustenuggee later recalled: "In council, it was determined to strike a decided blow about this time … It was determined that [Osceola] … should attack Fort King, in order to reach General [Wiley] Thompson, then return to the Wahoo Swamp, and participate in the assault meditated upon the soldiers coming from Fort Brooke …" (quoted in Sprague 1848: 90).

During the second day's march, Dade sent Pacheco ahead to assess the next crossing at the Hillsboro River, but the scout found the bridge a smoldering ruin. Besides a breastwork to protect the campsite that night, Dade ordered a raft built to float the six-pounder gun across the river. He also sent Private Aaron Jewell, Co. C, 2d Artillery, back to Fort Brooke to inform post commander Captain Francis S. Belton, 2d Artillery, of the burnt bridge and urge him to send supplies and reinforcements. Next morning the troops forded the river successfully, but the gun slipped off the raft and fell into the water. The gun was extricated after much difficulty and only after Private John Thomas, Co. B, 2d Artillery (temporarily transferred to Dade's command), had sustained a painful back injury and was ordered to make his way back to Fort Brooke.

Owing to problems with the river crossing, Dade's troops covered only 6 miles on December 25 before setting up a fortified camp in the Wahoo Swamp. Shortly after dark, Private Jewell re-joined the column after having left Fort Brooke that afternoon and brought news that reinforcements led by Major John Mountfort, 2d Artillery, would reach Dade the next morning. What Jewell did not know was that the vessel carrying Mountfort's equipage had dropped anchor in the wrong bay and would take several days to find its way along the coast to Fort Brooke. Mountfort's command would not be coming to the aid of Dade.

Sent ahead of the column on December 26 to reconnoiter the next river crossing, Pacheco found the bridge over the 50ft-wide Withlacoochee River only partially burned. After replacing some damaged planks, the troops crossed over and went into camp 2 miles beyond the river. The burning of bridges by the Seminoles must have seemed more malicious than strategic to Dade at this point, but Halpatter-Tustenuggee was buying time until his warriors could be joined by those under Chiefs Osceola and Micanopy, who it was planned would attack Fort King. Dade's command reached the Little Withlacoochee River during the next day and found the bridge there also burnt, but this narrower river provided less of an obstacle to cross. The troops were ordered to fell a tree for use as a makeshift footbridge as the horses once again dragged the gun through the stream. Their next fortified encampment was set up 4 miles beyond the Little Withlacoochee at Round Clay Sink.

Arriving at Fort Brooke on March 6, 1836, Ensign Alexander B. Meek of the Battalion of Alabama Volunteers described the post as a picket fort with two block houses. By 1842, the post had become the largest active military installation of the US Army, and served as a base for operations into the interior of Florida as well as a port of embarkation for moving Seminoles west. (Library of Congress: LC-DIG-pga-10851)

MAP KEY

1 *c.*0800hrs: Chief Micanopy gives the signal and the Seminoles open fire from the tall grass to the left of the road. Major Francis L. Dade, Captain Upton S. Fraser, and 2d Lieutenant Robert R. Mudge, plus most of the advance guard and some of the main column, fall dead or seriously wounded.

2 *c.*0801hrs: The Seminoles advance on the main column.

3 *c.*0801–0803hrs: US survivors in the main column take cover behind pine trees either side of the road and return fire.

4 *c.*0803–0900hrs: 2d Lieutenant William E. Basinger directs the unlimbering and loading of the six-pounder gun, which is discharged at the Seminoles during the next hour.

5 *c.*0900hrs: Driven back by the gunfire and stubborn musketry, the Seminoles withdraw about 1 mile to the northeast into the pine woods and palmettos.

6 *c.*0900–0945hrs: The remaining US troops hastily fell pine trees and build a triangular-shaped low breastwork, while others gather ammunition from their fallen comrades.

7 *c.*0945hrs: Discovering that some US troops had survived, the Seminoles renew their attack. Some troops defend the breastwork while others are still spread out behind the pine trunks. The Seminoles slowly surround the breastwork, forcing the few remaining troops to withdraw inside the breastwork during the next four hours of fighting.

8 *c.*1400hrs: The Seminoles charge the breastwork and kill all the remaining defenders except for three enlisted men who feign death.

Battlefield environment

As Dade's column marched along the King Highway military road toward Fort King on December 28, 1835, it passed an extensive area of pine woods, palmettos, and tall grass about 5ft high, and continued on past a thicker palmetto cluster on its left. In one of his accounts of the battle, survivor Private Ransom Clark wrote: "The ground seemed to me an open pine barren, no hammock near that I could see. On our right, and a little to our rear, was a large pond of water some distance off. All around us were heavy pine trees, very open, particularly towards the left, and abounding with long grass" (quoted in Cohen 1836: 70–71).

Published in 1848 in John L. Thomson's *History of the Second War between the United States and Great Britain*, this detail from an ornate engraving titled "Massacre of Major Dade's Detachment" depicts the closing stages of the action, and shows the remains of Dade's command making their last stand behind a log breastwork as the Seminoles close in. The capless man leaning against the breastwork at center may be a depiction of either 2d Lieutenant Richard Henderson or 2d Lieutenant John L. Keais, who had both arms broken and in a sling. (Internet Archive)

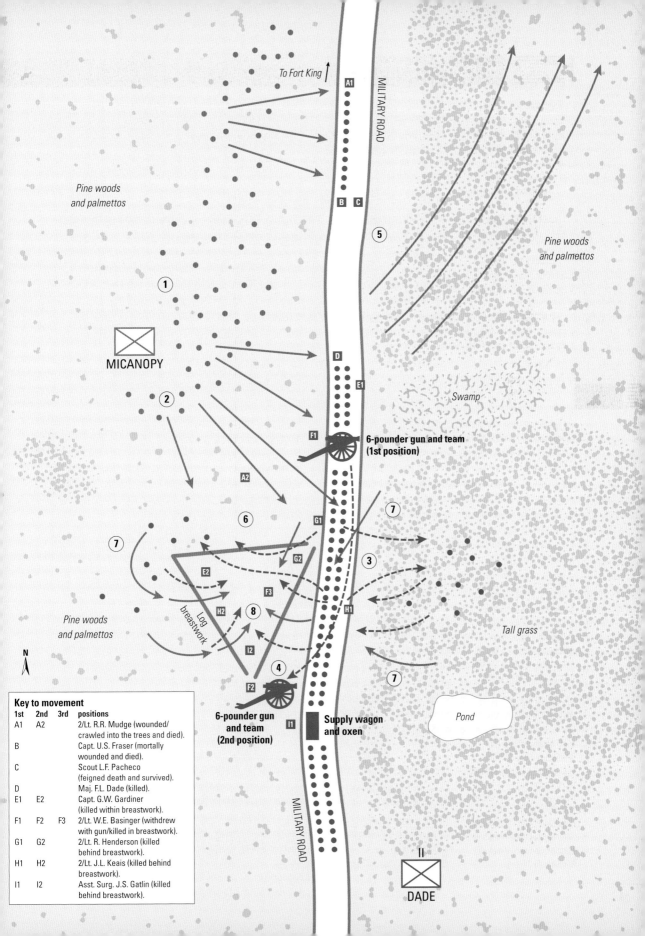

To Fort King

MILITARY ROAD

Pine woods
and palmettos

Pine woods
and palmettos

MICANOPY

Swamp

6-pounder gun and team
(1st position)

Log breastwork

Pine woods
and palmettos

N

Tall grass

6-pounder gun
and team
(2nd position)

Supply wagon
and oxen

Pond

MILITARY ROAD

DADE

Key to movement

1st	2nd	3rd	positions
A1	A2		2/Lt. R.R. Mudge (wounded/crawled into the trees and died).
B			Capt. U.S. Fraser (mortally wounded and died).
C			Scout L.F. Pacheco (feigned death and survived).
D			Maj. F.L. Dade (killed).
E1	E2		Capt. G.W. Gardiner (killed within breastwork).
F1	F2	F3	2/Lt. W.E. Basinger (withdrew with gun/killed in breastwork).
G1	G2		2/Lt. R. Henderson (killed behind breastwork).
H1	H2		2/Lt. J.L. Keais (killed behind breastwork).
I1	I2		Asst. Surg. J.S. Gatlin (killed behind breastwork).

INTO COMBAT

The soldiers of Dade's command awoke before dawn on December 28. The air was damp from the previous evening's light rain. Indeed, rain had been plaguing them all along the march. As they cooked breakfast under overcast skies, most believed that the danger was past because they were heading into open country where ambush would be more difficult. Not far away, the scene at the Seminole camp was one of intense excitement as the warriors danced to keep warm in the early morning cold.

Although the time had come for decisive action, there was hesitation in the Seminole ranks. Micanopy wanted to delay the attack until Osceola arrived as was planned, but Chief Otee Emathia, also known as Jumper or Leaping Tiger, reproached him for being timid. Addressing the warriors, Otee Emathia requested that those with faint heart should stay behind. As he and his followers prepared for the attack, Micanopy announced he would join them. Of the moments that followed, Halpatter-Tustenuggee recalled: "we moved out of the swamp into the pine-barren. I counted, by direction of Jumper, one hundred and eighty warriors. Upon approaching the road, each man chose his position on the west side; opposite, on the east side, there was a pond. Every warrior was protected by a tree, or secreted in the high palmettos" (quoted in Sprague 1848: 90).

As Dade's column moved along in a drizzling rain, they probably marched with their hands up the sleeves of their overcoats and with muskets slung or held across their arms. Through lack of vigilance by the officers and NCOs, many men had pulled on their overcoats and buttoned them up over their cartridge boxes and other accoutrements, making it difficult to reach for ammunition to load or reload their muskets. Furthermore, their commander seemed more relaxed. Having marched more than halfway to Fort King, through what was considered the most dangerous part of the route without being attacked at any of the four river crossings, Dade for the first time failed to post guards on the flanks. At about 0800hrs the rain stopped and the sun shone as the column marched out of the low country into an area of pine woods, palmettos, and tall grass.

The column had progressed about 3 miles, the advance guard of eight men about one-quarter mile ahead and marching in single file with 2d Lieutenant Robert R. Mudge, Co. B, 3d Artillery, riding in front, and Fraser and Pacheco at their rear. Dade and Gardiner led the main body of men in column of route with two files about 6ft apart. Behind them lumbered the six-pounder gun. The rear guard under 2d Lieutenant William E. Basinger, Co. C, 2d Artillery, escorted the supply wagon. The other two officers and Assistant Surgeon John S. Gatlin were spread throughout the column.

According to Clark, one of the three survivors of the attack, Major Dade turned in his saddle moments before the attack and announced, "We have now got through all danger – keep up good heart, and when we get to Fort King, I'll give you three days for Christmas" (*BMP*, June 6, 1837: 2:2).

Of the seconds hiding in the long sawgrass after the advance guard had passed by and the main column approached, Halpatter-Tustenuggee recalled:

In advance, some distance, was an officer on a horse, who, Micanopy said, was the captain; he knew him personally; had been his friend at Tampa. So soon as *all* the soldiers were opposite, between us and the pond, perhaps twenty yards off, Jumper gave a whoop, Micanopy fired the first rifle, the signal agreed upon, when every Indian arose and fired, which laid upon the ground, dead, more than half the white men. (Quoted in Sprague 1848: 90–91)

Recalling the moment of attack in the *Boston Morning Post* in 1837, Clark stated:

At this time we were in a path or trail on the border of the pond, and the first notice that we received of the presence of the enemy was the discharge of a rifle by their chief, as a signal to commence the attack. The pond was on our right, and the Indians were scattered round, in a semicircle, on our left, in the rear and in advance, reaching at the two latter points to the edge of the pond; but leaving an opening for our entrance on the path, and a similar opening on the other extremity for the egress of our advance guard, which was permitted to pass through without being fired on, and of course unconscious of the ambuscade through which they had marched. At the time of the attack this guard was a quarter of a mile in advance, the main body following in column two deep. (*BMP*, June 6, 1837: 2:2)

In an earlier statement published in 1836, Clark recalled:

It was 8 o'clock. Suddenly I heard a rifle shot in the direction of the advanced guard, and this was immediately followed by a musket shot from that quarter. Captain Fraser had rode by me a moment before in that direction. I never saw him afterwards. I had not time to think of the meaning of these shots, before a volley, as if from a thousand rifles, was poured in upon us from the front, and all along our left flank. I looked around me, and it seemed as if I was the only one left standing in the right wing. Neither could I, until several other vollies [*sic*] had been fired at us, see an enemy – and when I did, I could only see their heads and arms peering out from the long grass, far and near, and from behind the pine trees … The first fire of the Indians was the most destructive, seemingly killing or disabling one half our men. (Quoted in Cohen 1836: 70–71)

As a result of this first volley of fire Dade was knocked to the ground dead, following which his horse dashed into the midst of the Seminoles. Also killed or mortally wounded were Fraser and Mudge, plus several NCOs and privates.

This hand-colored lithograph of Osceola was produced by George Catlin (1796–1872) and was based on an earlier portrait he painted of the Seminole chief while he was gravely ill in Fort Moultrie, South Carolina, in January 1838. He depicts Osceola's elaborate wardrobe, which included a patterned turban with black and white plumes, patterned hunting shirt, and three silver gorgets around his neck, which were an intertribal mark of military rank derived from the British Army when Native Americans were under colonial rule. He is depicted armed with a flintlock musket and has a ball pouch and powder horn suspended over his shoulder. (National Portrait Gallery, Smithsonian Institution NPG.94.53)

Micanopy

Belonging to the Alachua Seminoles, Micanopy, or Crazy Alligator, was born c.1780. The grandson of King Payne, who is credited with uniting the Seminole as a people, he became Principal Chief and Governor of the Seminole Nation following the death of Bolek in 1819. In his *Notices of Florida* published in 1836, Myer M. Cohen, who served with the Regiment of South Carolina Volunteers in Florida, provided a not very flattering description of Micanopy as being of "low, stout, and gross stature, and what is called loggy in his movements – his face bloated and carbunkled, eyes heavy and dull, and with a mind like his person" (Cohen 1836: 238).

Although he attempted to negotiate a peaceful resolution between the Seminoles and local authorities, Micanopy had opposed the signing of the Treaty of Payne's Landing of 1832. Typical of elite Seminoles in the early part of the 19th century, he hired more than 100 fugitive slaves to work his estates and encouraged intermarriage between the Seminole and African Americans whom he considered to be his equal. Despite his age, he joined forces with the younger chiefs Osceola, Halpatter-Tustenuggee, and his nephew Coacoochee, or Wild Cat. Reluctantly becoming involved in the attacks on December 28, 1835, he fired the signal shot which began the massacre of Dade's column.

Despite further successful Seminole resistance in 1836, Micanopy became convinced of the futility of war against the unlimited manpower of the US. Having surrendered in June 1837, he began to negotiate moving to Indian Territory, but was kidnapped by Osceola. Despite having agreed to sign a peace treaty, he was captured by Jesup's forces while under a flag of truce in December 1838. Imprisoned at Charleston, South Carolina, Micanopy was eventually released and sent with around 200 other Seminoles to Indian Territory. He died aged about 69 at Fort Gibson on January 2, 1849.

This portrait of Micanopy was painted by Charles King Bird c.1826. (National Portrait Gallery, Smithsonian Institution; gift of Betty A. and Lloyd G. Schermer NPG.99.168.40)

Riding with the advance guard, Pacheco managed to survive the attack after pleading with the Seminoles for his life, and recalled:

Captain Frazier [*sic*] and I turned aside to examine an old gray horse we found by the road, and finding it worthless, had returned to the road, and had nearly overtaken the advance guard, when I heard a single rifle shot, and I looked back to see if someone was shooting game, but just in time to see Major Dade fall … shot in the breast. (*CJ*, August 1861)

The soldiers not killed or wounded by the first volley would have struggled to unbutton their overcoats in order to reach for cartridges to reload their muskets and bring them to bear. The sudden whooping and yelling of the Seminoles, the rifle and musket fire, and the cries of the wounded and dying would have been a shocking departure from the silence of seconds before. Continuing his narrative published in 1837, Clark wrote, "We promptly threw ourselves behind trees, and opened a sharp fire of musketry. I, for one, never fired without seeing my man, that is, head and shoulders – the Indians chiefly fired lying or squatting in the grass" (quoted in Cohen 1836: 71).

As the firing became more intense, Gardiner attempted to rally the scattered men while Basinger frantically directed the unlimbering,

Robert R. Mudge

Second Lieutenant Robert Rich Mudge was born in Lynn, Massachusetts on June 4, 1809, the oldest of 11 children. His father Benjamin Mudge, commander of a Lynn Artillery militia company, probably inspired his son to pursue a military career and at 17 years of age, Robert applied to the United States Military Academy at West Point, New York. Although the Academy denied his first two applications, in July 1829 he was accepted on his third attempt. He graduated from the Academy on July 1, 1833, and was attached to the 3d Artillery as brevet second lieutenant, being stationed at Fort Sullivan at Eastport, Maine.

Mudge was recalled to West Point as an assistant instructor in military tactics on October 23, 1834, and sometime after that made an excursion with several others to Montreal and Quebec, Canada, visiting the British officers in those places and examining their system of military discipline and tactics. On September 2, 1835, he was promoted to full second lieutenant and deployed to Florida where he was assigned to Co. B, 3d Artillery stationed at Fort Brooke.

He commanded the advance guard of Dade's column and was one of the first to be killed on December 28, 1835. Along with other US regular soldiers killed during the attack, his body was eventually interred at the St. Francis Barracks in St. Augustine, Florida. A concrete Endicott Period 3in M1898 gun battery located on Fort Armistead, Maryland, was named for Mudge via General Order No. 78, May 15, 1903. Battery Mudge was deactivated in 1920.

loading, and firing of the six-pounder gun. Owing to the haste of reacting to an ambush without proper time to place the gun in standard operations, the gun crew would have fired a quicker-loading 1¼lb powder charge at zero elevation, which would have resulted in an average range of 318yd – causing any solid shot to soar above the heads of the intended targets. More effective against the scattered Seminoles, the grapeshot fired spread out like a shotgun blast and did considerable damage. According to Halpatter-Tustenuggee, the gun was

> discharged several times, but the men who loaded it were shot down as soon as the smoke cleared away; the balls passed over our heads. The soldiers shouted and whooped, and the officers shook their swords and swore. There was a little man, a great brave, who shook his sword at the soldiers and said, "God-dam!" – no rifle ball could hit him. (Quoted in Sprague 1848: 91)

After about an hour of fighting the Seminoles were driven off by the gunfire and stubborn musketry of the surviving soldiers and fell back about a half-mile. Clark recalled that the six-pounder gun appeared "to frighten the Indians, and they retreated over a little hill to our left, one half or three-quarters of a mile off" (quoted in Cohen 1836: 71). Not wasting a second of this respite, Gardiner ordered the scattered wounded to be carried or dragged and laid

This portrait of Robert R. Mudge was produced by African-American lithographer John H. Bufford (1810–70), of Boston, Massachusetts, and is probably based on an earlier painting. (Internet Archive)

around the gun. Meanwhile, other soldiers were ordered to begin felling young pine trees with which to make a makeshift breastwork. A few men began searching among the dead and wounded for more ammunition. The breastwork was formed into interlocking layers about 2½ft tall forming a rough triangle around the gun. By this time there were only about 30 men left as Gardiner prepared to make a last stand defense, and Gatlin did what he could for the wounded and dying.

As he gathered cartridges, Clark found Mudge sitting with his back against a tree and evidently dying. Wounded by the first volley of Seminole fire while riding at the head of the advance guard, Mudge had crawled to join the main column, being wounded twice more in the process.

All remained quiet for about three-quarters of an hour after the Seminoles withdrew. Although mistakenly believing that all Dade's column was dead or dying, the Seminole scouts led by Otee Emathia and Halpatter-Tustenuggee became aware that some soldiers remained alive and they wished to finish them off. According to Halpatter-Tustenuggee:

> As we were returning to the swamp supposing all were dead, an Indian came up and said the white men were building a fort of logs. Jumper and myself, with ten warriors returned. As we approached we saw six men behind two logs placed one above another, with the cannon a short distance off. This they discharged at us several times, with the cannon a short distance off, but we avoided it by dodging behind trees just as they applied the fire. (Quoted in Sprague 1848: 90–91)

Not all, including Micanopy, were in agreement with continuing the action and it took derision and insults from the two chiefs, asking if their warriors were "drunk, sick or women to be afraid of a few white men," (quoted in Cohen 1836: 77), to persuade the Seminoles to launch a second attack. Of the commencement of the second attack, Clark recalled:

> We had barely raised our breastwork knee high, when we again saw the Indians advancing in great numbers over the hill to our left. They came on boldly till within a long musket shot, when they spread themselves from tree to tree to surround us. We immediately extended as Light Infantry, covering ourselves by the trees, and opening a brisk fire from cannon and musketry. The former I don't think could have done much mischief, the Indians were so scattered. (Quoted in Cohen 1836: 71)

In his *Boston Morning Post* account of events, Clark stated:

> A part of our troops fought within the breast-work, and a part outside. I remained outside till I received a ball in my right arm, and another near my right temple, which came out at the top of my head. I next received a shot in my thigh, which brought me down on my side, and I then got into the breast-work. (*BMP*, June 6, 1837: 2:2)

Toward the end of the battle, the only officers not killed or wounded were Gardiner, Basinger, and Gatlin. 2d Lieutenant Richard Henderson, Co. C, 2d Artillery, had his left arm broken, but continued to load and fire a musket.

He attempted to cheer and encourage the men until shot dead toward the end of the action. 2d Lieutenant John L. Keais, Co. B, 3d Artillery, had both arms shattered by musket balls during the first attack. Reclining behind the breastwork with both limbs in a sling, he remained oblivious to events swirling around him until tomahawked to death when the Seminoles finally overran the breastwork.

Gardiner received five or six shots before he fell, the mortal wound being in the breast. When he fell, Basinger attempted to encourage the few men that remained by shouting, "Now, my boys, let us do the best we can – I am the only officer left" (*NWR*, August 20, 1836: 420:1). Before meeting his death, Gatlin knelt behind the breastwork armed with two double-barrel guns and, according to Clark, was heard to say, "Well, I have got four barrels for them!" (quoted in Cohen 1836: 73). Of the closing stages of the battle, Clark recalled:

> Our men were by degrees all cut down. We had maintained a steady fight from 8 until 2 P.M. or thereabouts, and allowing three quarters of an hour interval between the first and second attack, had been pretty busily engaged for more than 5 hours. Lt B.[asinger] was the only officer left alive, and he severely wounded. He told me as the Indians approached to lay down and feign myself dead. I looked through the logs, and saw the savages approaching in great numbers. (Quoted in Cohen 1836: 72)

In his *Boston Morning Post* account of events, Clark added:

> I was about the last one who handled a gun, while laying on my side. At the close, I received a shot in my right shoulder, which passed into my lungs – the blood

The handwritten label on this artifact states, "A Seminole war plume picked up on Dade's Battleground by the late Colonel Alex R. Thompson, US Army, Florida. War Department, Rec'd Feb. 20th, 1845." It is doubtful that Thompson, who was later killed in action at Lake Okeechobee, retrieved this item as he was not with the column that discovered the remains of the Dade battle site on February 20, 1836. (Department of Anthropology, Smithsonian Institution: E034400-ant-02-201303)

gushed out of my mouth in a stream, and, dropping my musket, I rolled over on my face. The Indians then entered the breast-work, but found not one man standing to defend it. (*BMP*, June 6, 1837: 2:2)

Of these closing stages, Clark commented:

A heavy made Indian, of middle stature, painted down to the waist (corresponding in description to Miconope [*sic*]), seemed to be the Chief. He made them a speech, frequently pointing to the breastwork. At length, they charged into the work; there was none to offer resistance, and they did not seem to suspect the wounded being alive – offering no dignity, but stepping about carefully, quietly stripping off our accoutrements, and carrying away our arms. They then retired in a body in the direction from whence they came. (Quoted in Cohen 1836: 72)

Shortly after the warriors' withdrawal, a party of about 60 ex-slaves and allies of the Seminoles arrived on horseback and began stripping the dead soldiers, and cutting and mutilating all who showed any signs of life. According to Clark, who continued to feign death, they taunted the dead and dying soldiers whose government defended and maintained the slave trade with cries of "What have you got to sell?" (Cohen 1836: 72).

The battle was over and the field fell quiet after the African-American allies departed. Of the 108 soldiers and civilians in Dade's column on December 28, only three ultimately survived the massacre. As Clark crawled out of the breastwork and began to make his escape, he discovered that Private Edwin DeCourcey, Co. B, 2d Artillery, had also survived and the two men headed for Fort Brooke – even though Fort King was closer, neither man wanted to follow the departing Seminoles and their African-American allies north. Having been wounded five times, Clark was doubtless helped along by DeCourcey, but within a few hours they were spotted by a mounted Seminole warrior and hurriedly decided to split up. The Seminole pursued and killed DeCourcey but failed to find Clark and gave up the chase. Despite multiple wounds, Clark walked and crawled 65 miles back to Fort Brooke and was helped along toward the end of his three-day ordeal by a Native American woman. Arriving at the fort on December 31, 1835, he gave an account to Belton who immediately began fortifying the post in expectation of an imminent attack.

Another enlisted man to survive the massacre, 30-year-old Private Joseph Sprague, Co. B, 3d Artillery, also struggled back to Fort Brooke on his own and arrived on January 1, 1836. Although badly wounded, Sprague had also feigned death and climbed a tree (*WS*, June 28, 1836: 2:3; *BMP*, June 6, 1837: 2:2) before making his escape during the night following the battle. On his way back to the fort, he found a letter left on the trail by Fraser for Mountfort and brought it to the post. It stated: "beset by the enemy every night and we're pushing on" (quoted in Smith 1836: 38).

A third survivor was the Black scout and interpreter Pacheco, who was released from captivity by the Seminoles and also found his way back to Fort Brooke. Suspected by

This hand-colored engraving depicts Osceola's attack on the home of sutler Erastus Rogers at Fort King on December 28, 1835, during which Indian Agent Wiley Thompson and four others were killed. (North Wind Picture Archives/Alamy Stock Photo)

some of being a traitor and of betraying Dade and his command, he was held in confinement but eventually joined the thousands of Seminoles and their African-American allies transported to Indian Territory and survived until sometime around 1880.

The remaining part of the Seminole plan was enacted during the afternoon of December 28, 1835, when Osceola and 60 warriors descended on Fort King. They found Wiley Thompson and nine others dining at the house of the camp sutler, which stood about 250yd from the fort. Based on an account probably given by a Black cook who survived the attack, the *Charleston Mercury* reported:

> Rogers was setting [*sic*] at the head of his table, when the first intimation given of the presence of the foe, was a volley of, it is thought, at least 100 shot, poured in upon them through the open door. The Indians rushed upon the house. Those in, not killed, sprang out of it, at the windows on each side. Five, fleeing for Camp King, escaped. The others, fleeing for a hammock close by, were shot down. A negro woman, the cook … hiding behind a barrel, was unobserved by the Indians. They rushed into the house, Powell at their head, threw down the table, and looking around for a moment, left the house. The five of this party slain were, Gen. Thompson the Indian Agent, [First] Lieut. Constantine Smith [Co. F, 2d Artillery], Erastus Rogers the sutler, Suggs and Hitzler. Through Gen. Thompson were shot fifteen bullets, and sixteen through Rogers … All this was done in open day light, within 250 yards of Camp King – and in view of the 50 U.S. Troops, there at the time. (*CM*, January 12, 1836: 2:3)

The bodies of Dade's command lay where they fell on the battlefield for about two months until, on February 20, 1836, a column of about 1,000 men consisting of 450 regulars, plus some Louisiana militia and friendly Indians, commanded by Brevet Major General Gaines reached the site and buried the dead. In a letter written four days later, an officer in Gaines' column noted: "On our arrival at the battle-ground, we found the bodies of the dead lying generally as they were shot … I counted the skulls as they were thrown in, and there were 98 soldiers and 8 officers. The officers were recognized by different signs and marks about them. They were fully identified. Three graves were dug, and the bodies interred therein" (*NG*, March 11, 1836: 2:5).

The US Army dead as a result of the attack on Dade's column totaled seven officers and 96 enlisted men, plus an assistant surgeon and a servant. Estimates vary as to the number of Seminoles involved in the attack. According to 2d Lieutenant Woodburne Potter, 7th Infantry, who was on Gaines' staff and interviewed the survivors: "The force of the Indians could not have been less than three hundred and fifty men. This I judge from the extent of the ground they must have covered while in ambush. [Private John] Thomas estimated them at four hundred; [Private Ransom] Clarke's [*sic*] estimates vary from six hundred to one thousand; and [Private Joseph] Sprague thinks there were from five to eight hundred" (Potter 1836: 107). The most accurate estimate was probably that provided by Halpatter-Tustenuggee. Asked by Otee Emathia to count the number of braves involved prior to the attack, he counted 180 warriors. He also stated that only three warriors were killed and five wounded in the action (Sprague 1848: 90).

Unaware of the Dade Massacre, Brevet Major General Edmund P. Gaines, commanding the Western Military Department, marched a large force of regulars and volunteers inland to relieve Fort King. En route he discovered the site of the Dade's Massacre and ceremoniously buried the dead. On December 31, 1835, he fought the Seminoles at the Withlacoochee River, and was hit in the mouth by a spent rifle ball that knocked out several teeth. When relieved by a column led by Brevet Brigadier General Duncan L. Clinch, his men were near starvation and had been forced to eat horses and dogs. (Collection of Dr. William Schultz)

Lake Okeechobee, or Big Water

December 25, 1837

BACKGROUND TO BATTLE

The US response to the massacre of Dade's column was ineffectual as a series of ill-planned campaigns in 1836 led in turn by Brevet Major General Edmund Gaines, Major General Winfield Scott, and Governor Richard K. Call, failed to defeat the Seminoles. As a result, Major General Thomas S. Jesup, who helped subdue the Creek in Alabama and was still officially Quartermaster General of the US Army, was placed in command of the war in Florida on December 9 of that year. With over 9,000 men under his authority, which included elements of the US Navy and Marines, plus state volunteers, Jesup planned a major campaign using this much larger force.

With their limited manpower, the Seminoles could not compete against such odds. On January 27, 1837, a composite brigade of Army regulars, Marines, Georgia volunteers, and Native American allies commanded by Colonel Archibald Henderson, USMC, attacked a village along Hatchee Lustee Creek, capturing between 30 and 40 Seminole women and children, plus 100 pack ponies and 1,400 head of cattle. After other Seminole bands had been driven from the Withlacoochee River country, several Seminole chiefs surrendered and a truce was arranged toward the end of February. On March 6 a "Capitulation" (the Treaty of Fort Dade) was signed by a number of chiefs, including Micanopy, which stipulated that the Seminoles would be permitted to take their African-American allies west with them as their "property" (Mahon 1960: 200) rather than see them being taken back into white slavery. It soon became apparent, however, that this was not the case as white slave-owners began to seize back their "property." To hold Micanopy to his word, Jesup took a large band of hostages and held them in a Detention Camp near Fort Brooke. In retaliation, on June 2, 1837, Osceola and Chief

Abiaka, or Sam Jones, chief of the Miccosukee, a Seminole-Muscogee Creek tribe, led about 200 warriors in a daring raid on the camp and rescued Micanopy and about 700 other Seminoles and African Americans, and the war was on again.

Jesup decided to nullify the powerful force of opposition that Osceola represented. On numerous occasions in the past, Seminole chiefs had approached forts under flag of truce to be "fed and gifted" in return for a vague promise of emigrating. They then withdrew to "contemplate removal" with no intention of complying with any agreement, only to return at a later date expecting the same treatment. On October 21, 1837, Osceola was camped about 9 miles from Fort Brooke under flag of truce for the same purpose; but when he refused an outright demand to be removed west, he was surrounded and taken into custody along with about 80 lesser chiefs and warriors. Imprisoned in Fort Moultrie, opposite Charleston, South Carolina with 120 other warriors, plus 82 women and children, he died on January 30, 1838, from complications resulting from the effects of malaria and tonsillitis, which caused an abscess resulting in quinsy. His capture, along with that of Ee-mat-lá, or King Phillip, and his son Coacoochee, or Wild Cat, at Dunlawton Plantation earlier in the year, was a great loss to Abiaka, who now became the leader of Seminole resistance and was determined "to fight it out to the last" (*NNR*, February 10, 1838: 369:3).

During November 1837 Jesup began his main campaign with four columns, each of which entered the southern end of the peninsula from a different route, driving the Seminoles into the center of the Everglades and isolating them from any chance of outside assistance. Through constant campaigning and pressure on the food supply, Jesup hoped to end the war by March or April 1838. One column commanded by Brigadier General Joseph M. Hernández marched down the east coast from Mosquito South Lagoon and along the Indian River. A second column under Jesup moved south from Fort Mellon on Lake Munroe toward Lake Tohopkaliga and the Big Cypress Swamp. A third column led by Colonel Zachary Taylor proceeded east from Tampa Bay to Fort Gardiner near Cypress Lake, in preparation to proceed south along the Kissimmee River toward Lake Okeechobee. The fourth column under Colonel Persimor F. Smith marched up the Caloosahatchee River from the west coast toward Lake Okeechobee. Altogether a total of about 9,000 troops, the largest force used during the Second Seminole War, closed in on Abiaka and the remaining Seminole warriors gathered near Lake Okeechobee.

Before resorting to battle, Jesup sent four Cherokee mediators to parley with Abiaka in an attempt to persuade him to surrender and immigrate peacefully. At this time, the Seminole leader was injured after a fall from a horse and one of the mediators suggested he was weakening in his resolve to fight; but then, on the night of 29/30 November, Coacoochee and several others escaped from imprisonment in Fort Marion at St. Augustine and joined Abiaka's ranks, which lifted his spirits, and the mediators reported to Jesup that Coacoochee's escape had wrecked the plans for peace (Franke 1977: 46).

As a result, Jesup determined to do battle. On December 19, 1837, he directed Taylor to "proceed with the least possible delay" against any portion

Commanding the Eastern Department of the Army, Brevet Major General Winfield Scott was ordered to direct operations in Florida on January 21, 1836, with full authority to call upon the governors of South Carolina, Georgia, Alabama, and Florida for a militia force to support the small regular US Army. His elaborate campaign plan using a three-pronged attack to drive the Seminoles into the northern part of the territory failed partly due to a lack of co-operation with Gaines and Clinton, who were jealous of his appointment to command in Florida. Scott's strategy was also considered unsuitable to the wilds of a partially unmapped territory. On April 15, 1836, he was ordered north to quell a Creek uprising in Alabama. (Smithsonian National Portrait Gallery NPG.86.148)

An experienced US Army officer and friend of President Jackson, Governor of Florida Richard K. Call led several expeditions that failed to defeat the Seminoles. In November 1836 he led three columns into The Cove and forced the Seminoles to retreat, but they made a stand at Wahoo Swamp and once again escaped, leaving the US force exhausted and low on supplies. Disappointed in Call's performance, Jackson handed command of the war to Major General Thomas S. Jesup, Quartermaster General of the US Army. (Collection of the Museum of Florida History)

of the enemy he might find within "striking distance, and to destroy or capture him" (*NNR*, February 10, 1838: 369:3). Taylor detailed two officers and a small garrison composed of a detachment of the 2d Artillery to garrison Fort Gardiner, which he had established as a depot on the Kissimmee River. Taylor's force would be composed of elements of the 1st, 4th, and 6th Infantry regiments, plus a company of the 4th Artillery and a mounted unit of Missouri Volunteers, which included a detachment of scouts called "Morgan's Spies" made up of picked men from the regiment. Equipped with just a few wagons, Taylor was able to take with him only 12 days' rations.

Setting out at dawn on December 20, Taylor determined to drive the remaining Seminoles south toward the Everglades by marching his column along the west side of the Kissimmee River in a southeasterly direction toward Lake Istokpoga. Late on the evening of the first day's march, he encountered a party of 63 Seminoles led by Otee Emathia, who had led the attack on Dade's column and was the highest-ranking chief still in Florida. Described by 2d Lieutenant Robert C. Buchanan, Adjutant of the 4th Infantry, as being fit and healthy despite his advanced age (White & Buchanan 1950: 142), he had previously agreed with Taylor on December 7 to surrender and was taken under escort to Fort Fraser by some of the Shawnee scouts in preparation for migration.

During the morning of December 21, Taylor was joined by Captain Joseph Parks, an officer of Native American heritage who took command of the 70 Delaware Scouts accompanying the column. Taylor next sent three friendly Seminoles forward to gain intelligence regarding the location of the Seminoles led by Abiaka. At noon of the same day he ordered Lieutenant Colonel John W. Price to move several miles ahead of the main column with a battalion of the Missouri Volunteers to serve as an advance guard. Price was also to pick up any Seminole stragglers that might be found in their path.

About 2200hrs that evening, Taylor received a dispatch from Price stating that the Seminole scouts had returned with news that they had located a mostly deserted campsite 15 miles ahead which had been occupied by Halpatter-Tustenuggee and his band until four days ago. As a result, Taylor rode out with the remainder of the Missouri Volunteers to join Price at about 0300hrs, while ordering the infantry column in motion at dawn on December 22. He crossed a creek running out of Lake Istokpoga at about 1100hrs and reached the encampment by about 1400hrs which, according to Buchanan, was well situated on the edge of a thin pine wood and commanded a good view of a large prairie on either side (White & Buchanan 1950: 143). There he found 22 Seminoles consisting mainly of women and children, plus one old man who informed Taylor's interpreters that Abiaka and his warriors were about 20 miles away and ready for a fight.

At dawn on December 23, Taylor ordered the construction of "a small stockade work for the protection of a future depot" (*NNR*, February 10, 1838: 370:2), which was named Fort Basinger. In order that his column should move more quickly, he left his artillery and baggage train there under the command of Captain John Munroe's Co. G, 4th Artillery, with the pioneers, pontineers, and 85 sick and disabled infantry, plus a portion of the Delaware Scouts who claimed they "were unable to march further [*sic*]" (*NNR*, February 10, 1838:

Published in 1904 in Caroline Mays Brevard's *A History of Florida*, this engraving shows Osceola being arrested while under flag of truce at Fort Brooke on October 21, 1837. His imprisonment caused a national uproar, and the public condemned Jesup for violating a flag of truce. (Internet Archive)

370:2). The column moved out about 1400hrs, forded the Kissimmee River, and marched 7 miles before again going into camp.

Taylor continued his march at daybreak on December 24 with the captured old man as his guide, and proceeded in heavy rain over an extensive sodden prairie. By about 1000hrs the column approached a large campsite on the edge of a cabbage palm hammock, which the old man stated had recently been abandoned by Halpatter-Tustenuggee and several hundred Indians who had been slaughtering cattle. A few miles on, at a smaller hammock, some of Morgan's Spies surprised and surrounded four young Seminole warriors who waved a white flag. Professing to be friendly, they declared they were "preparing to come in" (*NNR*, February 10, 1838: 370:2). Of this encounter, Buchanan recorded in his diary that these Seminoles informed Taylor that Abiaka and his followers were encamped about 8 miles northeast in a large cypress hammock by a lake, and were ready to fight (White & Buchanan 1950: 144).

Setting the old man free, Taylor next used the young Seminole warriors as guides and around 1400–1500hrs reached a very dense cypress swamp. In anticipation of possible attack, he deployed his infantry in line of battle, and sent Morgan's Spies forward, accompanied by the Seminole guides, to pick their way through the swamp. As a result, two more Seminoles were captured who informed Parks that "a large body of Seminoles, headed by John Cochua, Co-a-coo-chee, and, no doubt, Alligator, with other chiefs," were encamped 5–6 miles farther away and, "near the Mickasukies [*sic*], with a cypress swamp and dense hammock between them and the latter" (*NNR*, February 10, 1838: 370:2). Once the column had crossed the swamp, and having marched about 16 miles that day, Taylor went into camp for the night.

Dwelling on the expected battle the next day, Buchanan expressed forebodings in his diary, wishing he could settle the matter in one blow with his greater force but anticipating a hard fight (White & Buchanan 1950: 144–45).

MAP KEY

1 *c.***1100hrs:** Colonel Zachary Taylor's column arrives about a half-mile from the hammock occupied by the Seminoles led by Abiaka. Taylor establishes a headquarters and camp in pine woods on dry land about three-quarters of a mile north of the hammock and holds a council of war. The Seminoles watch from the treetops and undergrowth of the hammock.

2 *c.***1200–1215hrs:** Taylor sends the mounted soldiers of Co. D and Co. K, 4th Infantry, under Captain George W. Allen, off to the right to reconnoiter. The Missouri Volunteers advance in column formation through the swamp toward the hammock, with Morgan's Spies at their head. The 6th Infantry and 4th Infantry advance 40yd behind them in column formation to the rear right and left respectively. The 1st Infantry remain in reserve near the campsite.

3 *c.***1230–1235hrs:** The Missourians are ordered into an extended skirmish line with Morgan's Spies, plus a small detachment of Co. D, 1st Infantry, and 30 Delaware Scouts, on their right wing. They advance to within 20yd of the hammock. The Seminoles open fire, breaking up the ranks of the Missourians.

4 *c.***1240hrs:** Although badly wounded, Colonel Robert Gentry and a small detachment of Missourians reach the dry ground of the hammock. Gentry is seriously wounded again and carried to the rear.

5 *c.***1240–1250hrs:** The 6th Infantry are ordered from close column into line of battle. The Seminoles fire a second volley,

which decimates the front line of this regiment. Captain Thomas Noel rallies the left wing and leads a charge into the hammock. The Miccosukee Seminoles under Abiaka fall back and begin to make their escape.

6 *c.***1255–1330hrs:** The 4th Infantry change from close column to line of battle and charge the hammock in open order. The regiment's right flank and rear are threatened by the Seminoles under Halpatter-Tustenuggee. Lieutenant Colonel William S. Foster orders a change of front, which brings the regiment around to face the enemy.

7 *c.***1330–1400hrs:** The Seminoles make three charges at this new front, which are all repulsed by a combined force of the 4th Infantry plus remnants of the 6th Infantry and the Missourians.

8 *c.***1400hrs:** The Seminoles under Coacoochee and Halpatter-Tustenuggee fall back and begin to make their escape.

9 *c.***1410hrs:** Taylor orders the two mounted companies of the 4th Infantry, having returned from their reconnaissance mission, to dismount and advance in support of the right wing of his troops in the hammock.

10 *c.***1420hrs:** Taylor orders the 1st Infantry under Lieutenant Colonel William Davenport forward to the left to complete the flanking of the right wing of those Seminoles remaining in the hammock.

Battlefield environment

When the army of Colonel Zachary Taylor approached Lake Okeechobee on December 25, 1837, it was confronted with a hammock defended by the Seminoles which was about 300yd in width and thick with cypress trees and an understory of bushes, bordered on three sides by a quagmire of swamp and sawgrass. About 300yd to the rear of the

Seminole lines was a sand ridge which ran along Lake Okeechobee's northeast shore, the open beaches of which furnished the Seminoles with avenues of escape if needed. For about 20yd ahead of the hammock the Seminoles had cut down the tall sawgrass and reeds in order to provide a more effective field for fire.

Published in 1837 in *Lithographs of Events in the Seminole War in Florida*, this lithograph entitled "Attack of the Seminoles on the Block House" depicts a block house built near the mouth of the Withlacoochee River during Scott's campaign in March 1836. Its small garrison of 45 Floridian militiamen came under siege for 48 days when it mistakenly did not receive orders to withdraw with the rest of the army. At a loss of only two killed and five wounded, the garrison was finally relieved after three volunteers slipped through the Seminole lines and paddled a canoe to the mouth of the Withlacoochee River and thence north along the coast to St. Marks. (Library of Congress: LC-DIG-ppsca-19924)

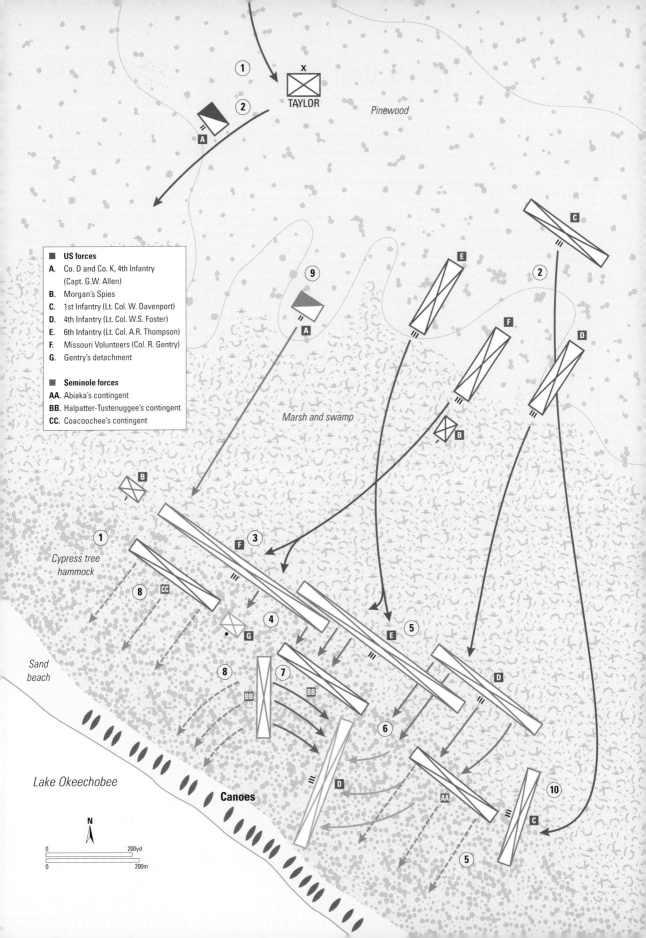

US forces
A. Co. D and Co. K, 4th Infantry
   (Capt. G.W. Allen)
B. Morgan's Spies
C. 1st Infantry (Lt. Col. W. Davenport)
D. 4th Infantry (Lt. Col. W.S. Foster)
E. 6th Infantry (Lt. Col. A.R. Thompson)
F. Missouri Volunteers (Col. R. Gentry)
G. Gentry's detachment

Seminole forces
AA. Abiaka's contingent
BB. Halpatter-Tustenuggee's contingent
CC. Coacoochee's contingent

TAYLOR

Pinewood

Marsh and swamp

Cypress tree
hammock

Sand
beach

Lake Okeechobee

Canoes

N

0   200yd

0   200m

INTO COMBAT

Taylor's column marched out of camp at daylight on December 25 and, after proceeding through pine woods for about 3 miles, reached a Seminole camp on the edge of another cypress swamp, which again must have contained several hundred people and bore traces of having been abandoned in a great hurry, as fires still burned. Formed in line of battle, the troops swept through the encampment. Emerging from the other side of the hammock, they were re-formed while many of them fired at random into nearby trees to make sure their muskets were still in working order and their powder had not been damaged by the damp (Monk 1978: 15).

In motion again by about 1100hrs, Taylor's troops reached a large prairie on which about 300 cattle and a number of Indian ponies grazed. At this point a mounted Seminole warrior was captured who identified himself as the brother-in-law of Black Seminole John Horse, or John Cavallo, who had escaped from Fort Marion with Coacoochee on the night of 29/30 November. According to Buchanan, when questioned the young warrior stated that the Seminoles, amounting to 2,000 men, women, and children, were in a large hammock about a half-mile away on Lake Okeechobee, and that among them 200 warriors were ready to do battle; he also warned that they had chosen a difficult place to attack (White & Buchanan 1950: 145). According to tradition among the Seminoles, this young warrior and possibly others captured earlier allowed themselves to be taken in order to guide Taylor's column into battle at a place of distinct advantage to Abiaka and his followers.

Abiaka had indeed chosen a great defensive position which would result in the largest pitched battle of the Second Seminole War. A quagmire of swamp made it a difficult place to approach and placed the advancing US troops in a most hazardous position even before they reached the firm ground of the dry hammock occupied by the Seminoles. An under-story of bushes provided cover for a line of well-armed gunmen who had notched the trees on which to steady their weapons. Above them, positioned in the tall trees, were lookouts and snipers. For about 20yd ahead the 5–6ft-high sawgrass and reeds had been cut down in order to provide a field for fire for the defenders.

Establishing a camp in pine woods on dry land about three-quarters of a mile north of the hammock, Taylor called his officers together and advised them of his plan of attack which involved a direct frontal assault, following which Colonel Robert Gentry proposed a flanking attack to the north or south (Monk 1978: 13). Gentry had observed that the hammock in which the Seminoles were hidden was only 300–400yd long, and stated that he believed cavalry as well as infantry could move across the swamp at either end and drive the Seminoles from one side to the other (Monk 1978: 14). He further pointed out that a direct attack across the open swamp would offer too great a target for the Seminoles, and that the troops, already worn out with their struggle through the deep mud, would not have sufficient energy left to fight once the hammock was reached. Taylor waited for Gentry to complete the outline of his alternative plan and then responded in a manner true to his usual way of dealing with militia, which he hated, by asking if Gentry was afraid to attack the center of the hammock through the swamp. Not wishing to be accused of cowardice, Gentry immediately confirmed that Taylor's orders would be carried out (Monk 1978: 14).

Through a field-glass Taylor could make out the smoke from the campsite within the hammock which the Seminoles were abandoning in great haste. He immediately deployed his troops for battle while they were still on firm ground. Commanding the two mounted companies of the 4th Infantry, Captain George W. Allen was ordered off to the right to reconnoiter. If no opponents were found and heavy firing was heard, he was to return to the campsite to rejoin Taylor.

Lieutenant Colonel Alexander G. Morgan formed the Morgan's Spies, numbering 43 men, at the head of a column formation. At a slight interval behind them stood the First Battalion of Missouri Volunteers commanded by Lieutenant Colonel John W. Price, consisting of three companies under Captains Congreve Jackson, William C. Pollard, and James Childs. Behind them stood the buglers and a standard-bearer holding aloft the regimental flag bearing the motto "Gird, gird, for the conflict, Our banner wave high; For our Country we live, For our Country we'll die" (quoted in Gentry 1918: 220). Immediately behind them was the Second Battalion, led by Major Harrison H. Hughes and composed of four companies under Captains Thomas D. Grant, John H. Curd, Cornelius Gilliam, and John Sconce. As 21 men were detailed as horse-handlers, and to guard the small baggage train in some dry pine woods, the battle strength of the Missourians was reduced from 153 to 132 men.

The regulars were about 40yd behind Hughes' battalion with the 6th Infantry led by Lieutenant Colonel Alexander R. Thompson forming the right column, and the 4th Infantry under Lieutenant Colonel William S. Foster slightly behind them forming the left column. Taylor's old regiment, the 1st Infantry, was held in reserve about 100yd farther back with Lieutenant Colonel William Davenport in command. The Missourians were ordered to receive the enemy's fire as they closed on the hammock, and in the event of the fire proving too severe, the line was to retire to the rear and form behind the regulars who were to press home the remainder of the attack.

Meanwhile, the Seminoles watched Taylor's little army from the within the dense foliage of the hammock. Near the center of their line was Halpatter-Tustenuggee with his own band of 120 warriors. On his left was Coacoochee with 80 more warriors, while on the right were nearly 200 Miccosukee Seminoles under Abiaka. Ten of his warriors covered themselves in Spanish moss for camouflage and climbed into the treetops to enable them to oversee

A career Army officer, Zachary Taylor was an experienced Indian fighter when he arrived in Florida in command of the 1st Infantry in 1837. Later nicknamed "Old Rough and Ready" because he was prepared to get his boots dirty alongside his men, he had a poor regard for volunteer soldiery and was criticized for reporting that the Missouri Mounted Infantry, which fought under him at Lake Okeechobee, had broken and fled when many of them fought as well as regulars. (National Portrait Gallery, Smithsonian Institution)

the advance of Taylor's troops, and communicate movements to those below. They also served as snipers. Commanding the Black combatants was John Horse. In their rear was Lake Okeechobee, with a clear sandy beach on which were a large number of canoes to facilitate escape when the time came to retreat. With Abiaka's command, the shaman Otolke-Thlocko was chanting and singing to instill courage in the young warriors, and this sounded eerily across the hammock toward Taylor's soldiers.

Beginning at about noon, the advance of Gentry's dismounted cavalrymen was difficult in the extreme. About a half-mile of swamp had to be crossed before the Missourians reached the hammock defended by the Seminoles. The depth of water, particularly on the left, made progress very slow, which would give the Seminole snipers plenty of time for careful and accurate fire. Claiborn Webb, a 22-year-old private in Childs' company, recalled: "We waded into the marsh, and were … in water that struck us between the waist and shoulder" (quoted in Gentry 1909: 102). After struggling slowly for about 200yd, Gentry halted to realign his sodden regiment. Some looked behind for support, but the regulars had still not moved. Halted again soon after, Gentry's men were relieved to see the 6th and 4th Infantry at last ordered forward.

After advancing a farther 300yd, the Missourians were ordered to break column and form into an extended skirmish line. Quartermaster Sergeant Thomas M. Bryant recalled that the swamp was covered with prairie sawgrass about 5ft high, and the ground was swampy and wet underfoot (Tucker 1991: 157).

With the standard-bearer by his side, Gentry splashed to the center and slightly ahead of the line. Removing his frock coat and rolling up the sleeves of his white shirt, he would make an ideal target for Seminole snipers waiting in the treetops. At the center was the First Battalion, Missouri Volunteers. On Gentry's left was the Second Battalion, Missouri Volunteers; on his right were Morgan's Spies, plus a small detachment of Co. D, 1st Infantry, and 30 Delaware Scouts led by Parks. According to a later report by Taylor, these friendly Native Americans played no part in the battle as they withdrew before suffering any casualties (Kersey & Petersen 1997: 454).

At about 1230hrs, Gentry raised his sword and bugles sounded the order to advance once more. As they floundered forward in the bright sunshine, the Missourians held their pistols, muskets, and cartridge boxes or powder horns as high as possible to keep them out of the water. There was no sign of life in the dark line of shadowy cypress trees as they approached nearer to the hammock. The only sound was the sloshing of water about their waists and legs, the sucking of mud in boots, and the occasional grunt as a man went down too deep in the mire.

At last the Missourians got to within about 20yd of the hammock. Many of them began to wonder if the Seminoles were still there, or whether they had abandoned yet another camp, when suddenly a withering fire burst from the undergrowth and treetops. In the first fierce volley almost 20 percent of the advancing force fell wounded or dead, and especially decimated was its left wing. Gentry was shot through the chest but, although badly wounded, the colonel remained on his feet and ordered his men to take cover. Not able to stand such murderous fire, however, some of the men bolted rearward; but the majority maintained reasonably good order and crouched as low as the water and mud would permit amid the cacophony of Seminole gunfire and shrill of

A veteran of the War of 1812, Richard Gentry was appointed a general in the Missouri State Militia about 1832. In 1837, he was requested to raise the 1st Missouri Volunteers to fight the Seminoles in Florida. Shot through the chest while leading the attack at Lake Okeechobee, he was assisted from the battlefield and might have survived had the surgeon not decided that his wound should be cleansed by pushing a silk scarf through it with a ramrod. He died just before midnight on December 25, 1837. (Portrait by George Caleb Bingham courtesy of St. Louis Art Museum)

turkey-bone whistles blown by the Seminoles. Webb recalled: "We were fired upon by the Indians, who were concealed in the brush upon the opposite bank, when our heads and shoulders were showing above the water. Many of us … stuck our heads beneath the water to prevent being a good target for an Indian bullet" (quoted in Gentry 1909: 102). At this point some troopers managed to catch a glimpse of the Seminoles who, Gilliam remembered, would rise from the dense growth of palmettos and fire with great accuracy (Tucker 1991: 160).

Still on his feet and attempting to urge on the remains of his regiment, Gentry seemed to realize that the only chance of survival in the face of such murderous fire was to gain the protection of the undergrowth in the hammock. As the assault began to dissolve into a series of fierce firefights, he led a small contingent in a desperate charge into the hammock. As he pushed into the undergrowth he was shot through the stomach at point-blank range and fell to the ground. The same ball, having passed through Gentry's body, is believed to have then impacted and shattered the arm of his 18-year-old son, Sergeant Major Richard Gentry, Jr., who was by his side. Elements of Curd's company, plus others of the Second Battalion, gathered protectively around their fallen commander and drove back several Seminoles who were intent on scalping him. Despite being twice wounded, Gentry begged to be lifted back to his feet so his men might not become dispirited and retreat.

Meanwhile, the regulars came up behind the Missourians. The five companies of the 175-strong 6th Infantry were ordered from column formation into a double line of battle and pushed on. The 4th Infantry moved toward their left and came up behind them in skirmish order. On its left wing, Buchanan recalled that the mud in the swamp was knee-deep, and that his regiment was exhausted before it reached the hammock (White & Buchanan 1950: 146). The 6th Infantry reached the area where the brush and most of the sawgrass had been cleared away. Completely without cover, they were now within rifle range of the hammock. Before ordering his regiment to open fire, Thompson shouted to the volunteers ahead of him not to advance any farther into the hammock. Commanding a company of Missourians in the battle, Lieutenant Colonel James C. Chiles recalled that his men "were obliged to stoop to avoid his fire" (*JCR*, March 31, 1838: 2:4).

Wisely deciding to concentrate on the 6th Infantry before the 4th Infantry also came into range, the Seminoles fired another volley, which exploded from the undergrowth and treetops, flew over the heads of the stricken Missourians, and crashed into the advancing regulars. Commanding Co. K, 6th Infantry, Captain Thomas Noel later wrote, "Our regiment went in immediately … and on approaching within rifle shot received a fire, but still pressed on" (*MA*, February 16, 1838: 2:2). The hail of lead was so deadly and accurate that many in the front rank of the regiment, which was shoulder-to-shoulder in close-order formation, were simply mown down and were dead, dying, or disabled.

In front of his regiment, Thompson was thrice wounded before he fell. The first ball passed through his abdomen, the second into his right breast, and the last through his chin and neck just as he was about to reach the edge of the hammock. According to an eyewitness, Thompson "fell in a sitting position and died instantly"; advancing next to him, regimental adjutant 1st Lieutenant John P. Center was "shot through the head from a tree, and died instantly" (*ANC*, February 1, 1838: 73:2). Commanding Co. F, Captain Joseph Van Swearingen was "shot in the neck, retired to the rear, raised both hands above his head, and fell flat upon his face, gave one groan, and was no more"; commanding Co. A, 1st Lieutenant Francis J. Brooke was "shot through the heart, and died with a smile on his face" (*ANC*, February 1, 1838: 73:2). Assuming command of what remained of the center and right wing of the 6th Infantry, Assistant Commissary of Subsistence Captain George Andrews suffered a shattered wrist, while regimental adjutant 1st Lieutenant William H.T. Walker was "literally shot to pieces; four balls passed through him, and several others grazed him"; amazingly, he was reported to be "fast recovering" by the end of January 1838 (*ANC*, February 1, 1838: 74:1).

Of the NCOs, Sergeant Major Henry Sleephack was shot in the abdomen and died two days later; Sergeant David Todd, Co. I, was killed; and Corporal Robert S. Kipp, Co. H, died of his wounds several days later. In his after-battle report, Taylor observed that when the 6th Infantry "retired a short distance, and were again formed," one of its companies had only "four men left untouched" by Seminole lead (*NNR*, February 10, 1838: 370:3).

Before the Seminoles opened fire on his regiment, Thompson had been concerned that it should maintain good order, and sent Noel to see that "the left companies should keep in line and preserve their directions on the center companies" (*MA*, February 16, 1838: 2:2). Of this part of the action Noel later wrote:

> After passing down the line, and rejoining my own company, Captain Andrews informed me he was wounded, and from loss of blood would have to retire (which he did). Not receiving orders and the men falling fast, I directed the three left companies to charge and enter the hammock, which was most gallantly done, under a most heavy and destructive fire, pushing our enemy before us. (*MA*, February 16, 1838: 2:2)

At this point the regulars were joined by about 14 of Gentry's Missourians under Gilliam and 1st Lieutenant John Blaky. Among the volunteers, Webb recalled "When we reached the water's edge the Indians were there to meet us. We turned loose on them with our rifles and then with our pistols, which proved very effective" (quoted in Gentry 1909: 102). Although sustaining further heavy casualties, the regulars and volunteers pushed into the hammock and the Seminoles began to give way. Establishing contact with part of the 4th Infantry, the men under Noel joined the right wing of that regiment throughout the rest of the battle.

As the 4th Infantry approached the edge of the hammock in open order, Foster yelled and swore at his regiment as it charged out of the water and engaged the Seminoles at close quarters. As the left wing of the regiment entered the trees, it was attacked in the flank, but Brevet Major William M. Graham ordered Co. B and Co. C under 1st Lieutenant Richard B. Scriven to change front to the left. With bayonets glinting, they met and drove the Seminoles across a creek that traversed the hammock.

As the body of the 4th Infantry moved on in line it was threatened in the rear and right flank by warriors under Abiaka. Reacting quickly, Buchanan reported this development to Foster, who immediately ordered a change of front which slowly brought the regiment round to face the enemy. Recording this event in his diary, Buchanan wrote that the Seminoles charged three times after the change of front (White & Buchanan 1950: 147). During the second charge, and due to the confusion of battle, Foster and a number of his men mistook them for their Delaware allies and dropped their guard, which allowed the Seminoles to open fire, wounding several infantrymen. Realizing his mistake, Foster rallied his troops and ordered them to push on, which cleared that part of the hammock. As the Seminoles attempted a third counterattack, the remains of two companies of the 6th Infantry reinforced Foster's command from the left and the remaining Seminole resistance began to crumble away.

By this time the Seminoles generally were losing the will to fight. According to Coacoochee, not an Indian on their left wing faltered until the US infantry closed in on them "whooping and yelling" (Sprague 1848: 214). Those on the right wing under Abiaka did not hold their ground as well, however, and earlier on began to waver and flee to the rear, escaping across Lake Okeechobee in their canoes. Eventually, the warriors under both Coacoochee and Halpatter-Tustenuggee found themselves pressed so closely they had no time to re-load and also began to fall back (Sprague 1848: 214). The powerful medicine of Otolke-Thlocko had not protected them from the enemy's bayonets or his musket balls.

Three US Army buttons dug at Fort Brooke in Tampa, Florida, between 1974 and 1988. Top: This one-piece "eagle" button with shield at left was originally attached to a Pattern 1839 forage cap. Center: Introduced in 1820 and in use until at least 1839, this one-piece greatcoat button displays the letters "U.S." with spread eagle above and oval wreath below. In its original state this would have been made of white metal or silver. Bottom: This two-piece "eagle" button with "A" in a shield was worn on the cuff of an artilleryman's jacket. (Author's collection)

The 4th Infantry at Lake Okeechobee

Viewed through the eyes of a Seminole warrior, the 4th Infantry change front in the hammock to counter a flank attack toward the end of the battle at Lake Okeechobee. 2d Lieutenant Buchanan yells the orders "Battalion half wheel to the right, on left platoon" and "Form a line" at the enlisted men and they move round to the right to face the charging Seminoles. Changing front was a difficult maneuver to perform under fire, especially in such difficult terrain, and some of the infantrymen shown here stumble over tree roots and through the tangled undergrowth in their effort to keep the battle line in order to face the enemy. Several men fall wounded while others lunge their fixed bayonets at Seminole warriors attempting to engage with them at close quarters. Of these events, Buchanan recorded in his diary that the 4th Infantry saved the day by this maneuver, which resulted in the Seminoles abandoning the field of battle (White & Buchanan 1950: 147).

Dressed for fight and then possible flight rather than being stripped for battle, the Seminole warriors wear hunting shirts or long shirts, leggings and moccasins, and wool turbans with feather plumes. Their weaponry consists of Indian Trade rifles and captured Model 1816 smoothbore flintlock muskets, plus clubs, tomahawks, and knives. Several are armed with bows and arrows.

Observing the turning tide of battle, Taylor next ordered forward Allen's two mounted companies of the 4th Infantry who had re-joined him after completing their reconnaissance ride to the right without contacting the enemy. They advanced dismounted to support the right wing of what remained of the 6th Infantry. Finally, Taylor ordered Davenport to lead the 1st Infantry off farther to the left to complete the flanking and turning of the enemy's right wing. The fresh regulars met with little opposition although two men were wounded. According to Buchanan, when the firing was nearly over the 1st Infantry was ordered to advance into the hammock but the regiment was too late to have any effect on the outcome (White & Buchanan 1950: 147).

The main fighting ended shortly after 1500hrs. Most of Taylor's troops were utterly exhausted, having fought their way through a muddy swamp for about three hours, and made little attempt to pursue the fleeing Seminoles as they scattered out of the hammock, across the sand ridge, and into canoes lying on the open sandy beach beyond. Buchanan recalled that Taylor ordered a withdrawal from the hammock about sunset and his exhausted troops found great difficulty bringing out the bodies of their fallen comrades. Establishing an encampment on dry ground beyond the sawgrass, they tended 112 wounded and buried 26 dead (White & Buchanan 1950: 147–48). Meanwhile, 11 Seminoles lay dead in the hammock and 14 wounded managed to escape.

According to Coacoochee, the next day the Seminoles scattered throughout the country in parties of ten and 15, and Abiaka moved into the Everglades on the Atlantic coast (West 2016: 389). After burying their dead and tending the wounded, Taylor's command marched north on December 27 to rejoin Munroe's small garrison at Fort Basinger and finally reached the greater protection of Fort Gardiner two days later. After resting his men and horses for several days, Taylor took the field again, marching south to link up with Jesup as soon as possible. On January 8, 1838, a report about the battle at Lake Okeechobee in the *Daily National Intelligencer*, of Washington, DC, concluded, "From signs in the sand, supposed to be by Alligator, and which the interpreter Abraham has seen, the latter gives it as his opinion that the Indians intended to war to the death."

The Loxahatchee River, or Turtle River

January 24, 1838

BACKGROUND TO BATTLE

A preliminary action to the final large-scale battle of the Second Seminole War took place three weeks after the encounter at Lake Okeechobee. On January 15, 1838, Lieutenant Levin M. Powell, USN, led a boat expedition from Fort Pierce, on the east coast, consisting of 80 sailors and soldiers into Jupiter Inlet and along the Loxahatchee River to locate sites for future forts and search of Seminole villages.

Landing on the south side of the river, Powell left 23 men to guard the boats and divided his force into two divisions led by Acting Lieutenant William P. McArthur, USN, and Acting Lieutenant Horace N. Harrison, USN, while 1st Lieutenant Henry W. Fowler commanded 25 men of Co. I, 1st Artillery (*NNR*, February 10, 1838: 383:2). Finding a fresh trail, they encountered a large herd of cattle and horses, among which they discovered a Seminole woman and learned from her that several Seminole villages were close by. Using her as a guide, they marched about 5 miles until they reached a wider beaten trail at the head of a cypress swamp, at which point they heard a war-whoop and came under fire.

This carbon photograph of Major General Thomas S. Jesup by Allen & Rowell of Boston was published in 1887. Still officially Quartermaster General of the US Army, Jesup was placed in command of the war in Florida on December 9, 1836. (Author's collection)

With his men extended in line of battle, Powell ordered a charge but the Seminoles, numbering about 80 warriors led by Chiefs Tuskegee and Halleck-Hajo, fell back about 800yd into a dense cypress swamp to make a stand. In the first exchange of fire, Lieutenants Powell, McArthur, and Harrison were all wounded and Navy acting surgeon Dr. Frederick Leitner was killed. The loss of the officers caused most of the sailors, who were raw undisciplined hands, to panic and fall back in disorder. With evening closing in, and with no prospect of being able to carry to the boats more wounded than they already had, the order was given to retire.

A disciplined rearguard action was fought by the regulars under Fowler and, when he was wounded, ex-Army officer and future Confederate General Joseph E. Johnston, who had accompanied the expedition as a civilian topographical engineer and acting adjutant, took command. When Powell's force finally returned to their boats, Johnston was the last to embark after his scalp had been grazed by a rifle ball. Having sustained five killed and 22 wounded, the expedition returned to Fort Pierce during the early hours of January 16 with one boat, containing gunpowder and alcohol, being accidentally left behind in the dark. Determined to punish the Seminoles responsible for repulsing Powell's expedition, Major General Jesup issued orders for the 2d Dragoons, composed of 600 men under Colonel William S. Harney, to march toward the Loxahatchee River the next morning.

Forced to march inland to get around the St. Lucie River, the column reached Camp Lloyd on January 18, 1838. Accompanying Jesup, Assistant Surgeon Jacob Rhett Motte described the column's route through the Halpatiokee Swamp as it headed west as a wide and unbroken expanse of water and morass interrupted only by tall, rank sawgrass, presenting a picture of "universal desolation" (Sunderman 1953: 186).

At Camp Lloyd, Jesup's column joined forces with the command of Brigadier General Abraham Eustis. Having marched about 200 miles from Fort Mellon, this consisted of ten companies of the 3d and 4th Artillery, 500 Tennessean and Alabamian volunteers, and a train of ambulances and baggage wagons. Proceeding southeast, the whole force moved back toward the coast and the Powell battlefield on January 19. The artillery, wagons, and pack mules formed the center column while the dragoons marched in single file at 100yd distance on the right flank, with the volunteers at a similar distance on the left flank. The men and animals hauled and pushed their way through

Suspended from a white buff-leather shoulder sling, the Pattern 1828 cartridge box had a decorative outer flap with impressed floral border and an oval at the center within which was set an eagle with "U" at left and "S" at right. A scroll above this bore the motto "E PLURIBUS UNUM" ("from many, one"). This pattern began to be replaced by a cartridge box with a plain flap during 1836. (Don Troiani)

the swampland with sawgrass tearing the legs of both men and animals and wagon wheels miring down in the thick mud. Of the end of that day's march, Motte wrote: "Our course … lay through a scattering growth of dwarf pine, and under-brush of saw-palmetto; and we encamped at night in the vicinity of a marshy bog, – partly in it. Our fatigue, however, rendered us indifferent as to where we lay our wearied limbs, and acheing [*sic*] heads; the foulest ditch would have proved a bed of hops" (Sunderman 1953: 188). During the course of the night, Jesup was joined by the 35 Delaware Scouts who had served under Taylor at Lake Okeechobee.

Encountering a river, which was probably the Halpatiokee, during the march around noon on January 20, Jesup ordered the column to go into camp on the edge of a hammock while the corps of pioneers under 1st Lieutenant Robert Anderson, Co. D, 3d Artillery, built a bridge overnight. Anderson would later become a hero in the North for his defense of Fort Sumter in Charleston Harbor on April 12–13, 1861.

After continuing south through the watery wilderness for the next two days, Jesup's column crossed the head of the St. Lucie River, following which they encountered an extensive Seminole campsite that showed signs of having recently been abandoned. Also noted were numerous well-beaten Seminole trails, all leading south. During the night of January 23, Jesup ordered signal rockets to be sent up in an effort to make contact with Taylor's column, which was marching on a parallel course farther west, but the rockets went unanswered.

MAP KEY

1 *c.***1200–1215hrs:** The advance guard consisting of Co. B, 2d Dragoons, commanded by Captain William M. Fulton, are fired on by a large body of Seminoles as they enter a dense hammock about 4 miles ahead of the main US column. The dragoons withdraw and inform Major General Jesup.

2 *c.***1220–1230hrs:** Jesup deploys his troops to launch an attack on the hammock with the 2d Dragoons and North Alabama Volunteers on the right, the 3d Artillery in two battalions at the center, and the Tennessee Mounted Infantry on the left. Co. B, 4th Artillery place their guns and Congreve rocket battery on dry ground in the rear, with Co. D and Co. G, 4th Artillery, acting as covering infantry.

3 *c.***1240–1330hrs:** The US troops struggle across the marsh toward the hammock with the Tennessean volunteers and dragoons in advance and 3d Artillery 25yd behind the Tennesseans. The artillery and Congreve battery fire shot and rockets over the heads of the advancing troops and into the hammock. The Seminoles on the right flank open fire when the Tennesseans are within 50yd.

4 *c.***1330–1335hrs:** The Tennesseans begin to waver and Jesup rallies them and attempts to lead a charge into the hammock. He reaches the west bank of the Loxahatchee River only to find himself alone. He is shot and wounded and withdraws to join the 3d Artillery as they enter the hammock.

5 *c.***1335–1345hrs:** All the Seminoles withdraw across the river to the east bank as the 3d Artillery advance into the hammock.

6 *c.***1345–1350hrs:** Elements of the 3d Artillery encounter the river and attempt to swim across it.

7 *c.***1350–1400hrs:** The 2d Dragoons ford the river farther upstream and outflank the Seminoles, who retreat east out of the hammock.

8 *c.***1415hrs:** The US troops emerge from the east side of the hammock and find an abandoned Seminole encampment. Elements of the 3d Artillery, commanded by 1st Lieutenant Robert Anderson and 2d Lieutenant William B. Davidson, advance in pursuit of the retreating Seminoles several miles beyond the hammock.

Battlefield environment

In the last pitched battle of the Second Seminole War, the Seminoles led by Chiefs Tuskegee and Halleck-Hajo placed themselves in a dense cypress-tree hammock through which the Loxahatchee River ran. In order to attack them, the army of Major General Thomas S. Jesup had to cross a half-mile of marsh with mud and water about 4ft deep in places. The Seminoles had cleared away some of the trees and sawgrass to give them a clear view of the US troops as they approached. They had also fortified and camouflaged themselves by forming screens of palmetto fronds and cutting notches in tree limbs in order to facilitate a steady and accurate fire.

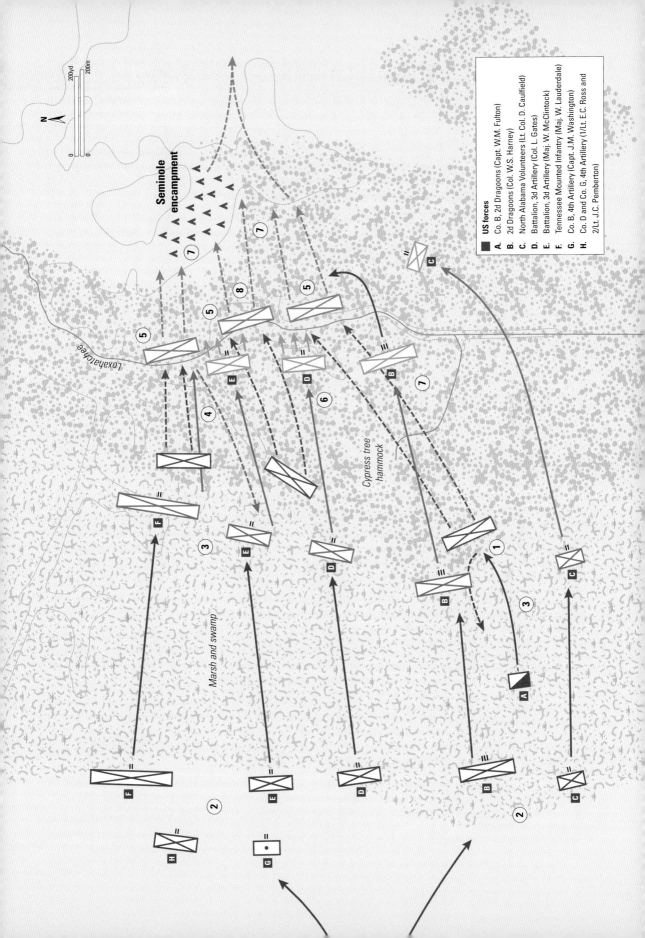

Seminole encampment

Loxahatchee

Cypress tree hammock

Marsh and swamp

N

200yd
200m
0
0

US forces

A. Co. B, 2d Dragoons (Capt. W.M. Fulton)
B. 2d Dragoons (Col. W.S. Harney)
C. North Alabama Volunteers (Lt. Col. D. Caulfield)
D. Battalion, 3d Artillery (Col. L. Gates)
E. Battalion, 3d Artillery (Maj. W. McClintock)
F. Tennessee Mounted Infantry (Maj. W. Lauderdale)
G. Co. B, 4th Artillery (Capt. J.M. Washington)
H. Co. D and Co. G, 4th Artillery (1/Lt. E.C. Ross and 2/Lt. J.C. Pemberton)

INTO COMBAT

Resuming his march on January 24, Jesup was informed around noon by his advance guard, commanded by Captain William M. Fulton, Co. B, 2d Dragoons, that a large body of Seminoles had been encountered in a dense hammock about 4 miles ahead. Opening fire just as Fulton's men were about to enter the tree line, the Seminoles, numbering about 300 warriors, wounded one horse and forced the dragoons into a hasty withdrawal. Jesup immediately ordered his troops forward. The news correspondent for the New York *Commercial Advertiser* accompanying the column recalled of the start of the action: "The dragoons and mounted men, mostly Tennesseans, immediately set off, and the artillery advanced as quickly as possible" (*ANC*, March 11, 1838: 159). According to Motte:

> We were not slow in obeying; and soon the palmetto bushes and scrub were making a tremendous cracking, as "rushed our steeds to battle driven" ... We quickly arrived in sight of the hammock where the Indians had posted themselves, and were awaiting us. In front was an almost impassable cypress slough, nearly half a mile wide; in passing through which we were up to our saddle girths in mud and water, our horses constantly stumbling over the cypress knees. (Sunderman 1953: 194)

As at Lake Okeechobee, the Seminoles held a strong position in a hammock, which on this occasion was spread over either side of the Loxahatchee River. All Jesup wrote in his brief official report of their deployment was that "the enemy was found there in an almost impregnable position" (*NNR*, February 17, 1838, 385:2–3). One of the Alabamian volunteers later recalled of the strength of the Seminole defensive position: "They had holes morticed in the trees, pickets set up, and palmettoes set up so as to cover them, and form blinds, and had cleared away the hammock on the side Jessup [*sic*] attacked them, which exposed his men altogether, without their seeing the enemy" (*CD*, February 24, 1838: 3:1).

The battle line was immediately formed by Jesup with Harney's 2d Dragoons and the North Alabama Volunteers, commanded by Lieutenant Colonel David Caulfield, forming the right flank, while the 3d Artillery, under Colonel Lemuel Gates, occupied the center, and the Tennessee Mounted Infantry, led by Major William Lauderdale, formed the left flank. Gates was at the head of the First Battalion, and Major William McClintock commanded the Second Battalion, 3d Artillery. Serving as mounted light artillery under Captain John M. Washington, Co. B, 4th Artillery unlimbered their six-pounder guns, howitzer, and Congreve rocket battery, and prepared to fire. Co. D and Co. G, 4th Artillery, commanded by 1st Lieutenant Edward C. Ross and 2d Lieutenant John C. Pemberton respectively, were ordered to protect the battery and formed in the rear. A future Confederate general, Pemberton would later complain that he never saw an Indian during his service in Florida. As they were deployed, all the dragoons, Tennesseans, and Alabamians were ordered to dismount and leave their horses in the care of one man to every seven mounts.

Advancing through the thick black watery mud toward the hammock, the regulars and volunteers engaged in an action which lasted about 40 minutes. Struggling and floundering over slippery cypress roots, they slowly approached the hammock until they were met by a flash of rifle fire and a blood-curdling war-whoop from the depths of the undergrowth facing them. A witness to this stage in the struggle, the news correspondent accompanying Jesup's command, recalled:

> When I came up I found them hotly engaged. We had a six pounder and howitzer, throwing grape, shells, and congreve [sic] rockets into the densest part of the hammock – if such there could be, where every part was so thick that a man could not see three feet ahead of him – while the Tennesseans entered on the left flank, the dragoons on the right, and the artillery in the centre. (ANC, March 11, 1838: 159)

Deployed too far to the right, the Alabamian volunteers took no part in the action at this stage. Of the advance of Gate's regiment, Motte recalled: "The Artillery soon came up, and joined in the conflict; some entering the hammock, which was so thick a man could not see two feet ahead of him ..." (Sunderman 1953: 194). Some of the Tennessean volunteers began to waver and held back from charging in the face of the fierce fire, at which point Jesup determined to rally and lead them forward. According to Motte:

> ... seizing a pistol in hand he dismounted from his horse and ordered them to follow him immediately. Saying this, he rushed forward into the hammock; and on reaching the edge of the stream, stopped and looked around to ascertain if he had been obeyed. He found himself alone; and at the same instant a ball struck him in the face, breaking his spectacles, and laying open the left cheek just below the eye. He picked up the pieces of broken spectacles and retired; his high opinion of the efficiency of volunteers, which had been previously exhalted [sic], very much lowered. (Sunderman 1953: 195)

Giving way, the Seminoles crossed by way of a ford to their main position on the east bank of the Loxahatchee, a fast-flowing river which would next present a major obstacle for Jesup and his troops. According to Motte:

> On gaining the centre of the hammock, we found a rapid and deep stream flowing between us and the Indians, who were delivering a deadly fire from behind trees on the opposite bank. The stream was about thirty yards in width; nothing daunted by this obstacle, our men hesitated not a moment, but plunged into the swift torrent, and crossed in the face of a shower of balls which whistled about their ears. The stream proved deeper than was anticipated; and many could only reach the opposite side by swimming. Such unexpected conduct indirect opposition to their own mode of proceedure [sic] so astonished the savages, that they immediately 'absquatulated.' And well it was for the men that they did so, their guns being useless without ammunition, which had been spoiled by the water, while they were swimming the stream. (Sunderman 1953: 194–95)

Meanwhile, being under less severe fire at the southern end of the battle line, Colonel Harney led 15 dragoons across the river farther upstream of

Dating from before 1842, this Seminole/Creek bandolier bag is said to have been found on a battlefield. The bandolier and pouch are of red wool strouding, edged with ribbon, enriched with elaborate beadwork, and lined with blue trade cloth. (Department of Anthropology, Smithsonian Institution: E391947_ant-01-201309/ E391947_ant-03-201309)

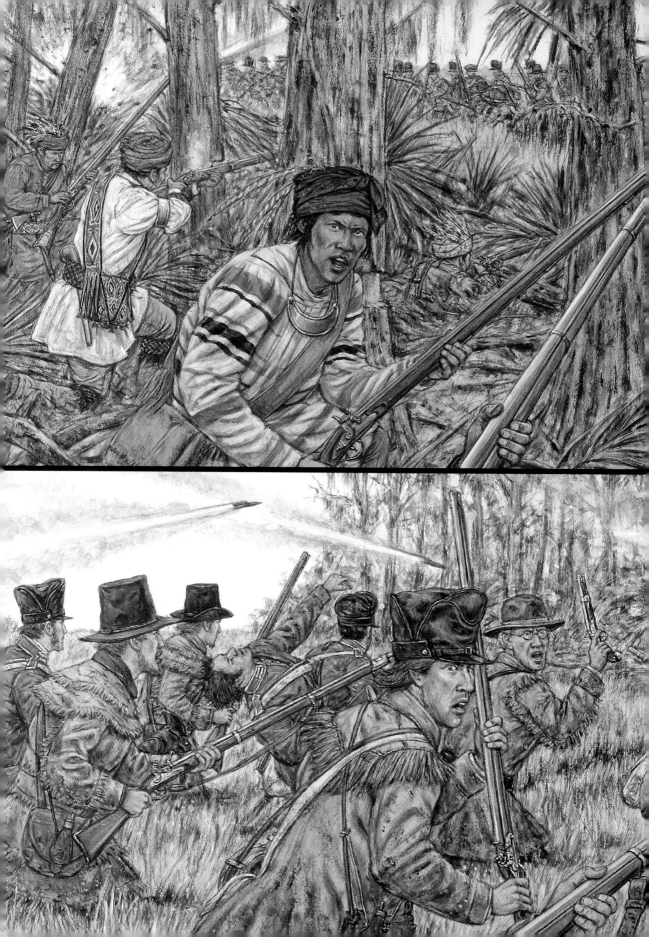

"No small racket" at the Loxahatchee River

Seminole view: Concealed behind a breastwork of cut-down tree limbs and palmetto fronds within a "woodland fortress" of evergreens, the Seminole warriors led by Tuskegee and Halleck-Hajo open fire as US troops struggle through the swamp toward them. To steady their aim, several warriors have rested their smoothbore Indian Trade muskets in notches cut in tree limbs. Others perch above in the trees using palm fronds to conceal their position. Their view of the advancing enemy is excellent across the area of swamp where they have cut down the sawgrass for about 50yd to their west. The main US attack force in the Seminoles' musket sights is Colonel Lemuel Gates' 3d Artillery in yellow-trimmed sky-blue jackets mixed with civilian clothing. The sky behind the advancing troops is filled with the flaming trails of Congreve rockets and smoke from the six-pounder guns as their lethal projectiles arc overhead and smash into the interior of the hammock behind them.

US Army view: As they approach the western edge of the hammock in front of the Loxahatchee River, the US troops led by Major General Thomas S. Jesup see nothing of the Seminoles waiting in the thick vegetation until they open fire. One of the Alabamian volunteers later recalled that the Seminoles had cleared away the sawgrass, which exposed his men altogether, without their seeing the enemy (*CD*, February 24, 1838: 3:1). Smoke and flames belch forth from all points in front of them, and musket balls rip through their ranks, knocking many down into the black swampy water. As the exultant Seminoles whoop and shriek, and the Congreve rockets and cannon shot scream over their heads, the 3d Artillery and 2d Dragoons press on at the center and right, while on their left the Tennessean volunteers panic and begin to flee. Waving a single-shot pistol in the air, Jesup attempts to rally them as black-powder smoke drifts across from the cypress trees and cabbage palm palmettos, and the Seminoles reload in preparation to deliver a second volley.

the Seminoles and managed to outflank their position. Seemingly unaware of the importance of the role played by Harney, Motte later entered in his diary: "As soon as we gained the opposite side of the stream … the enemy scattered up and down the hammock in the greatest alarm; and ceasing their yells soon disappeared altogether" (Sunderman 1953: 195). In his very brief official report of the battle, Jesup makes no mention of being wounded or of the dragoon commander's action in dislodging the Seminoles, but in a letter written to Secretary of War Joel Poinsett dated January 26, 1838, he explicitly mentioned Harney's flanking maneuver (Procyk 1999: 80–81).

Emerging into the open pine woods on the east side of the hammock, Jesup's troops found themselves in the midst of the Seminole camp where many of them had abandoned their packs and chattels. Close by they also discovered the remains of one of Lieutenant Powell's sailors lying as he fell nine days ago, with a bullet hole through his skull, which had been divested of its scalp. This proved to Jesup that he was on, or very close to, the earlier battle ground and had probably encountered and bested the Seminoles responsible for Powell's defeat. Determined to continue the action and overtake the retreating enemy, elements of the 3d Artillery, commanded by 1st Lieutenant Robert Anderson (Co. D) and 2d Lieutenant William B. Davidson (Co. F), advanced several miles beyond the hammock in pursuit of the Seminoles; their prolonged absence led to concern, according to Motte, that they had become casualties until they reported back later (Sunderman 1953: 197).

Regarding the number of killed and wounded in Jesup's command, Assistant Surgeon Nathan S. Jarvis stated in his diary that they had "killed in the engagement two, and seven wounded of the artillery, and five killed and twenty-three wounded of the Tennesseans; four of the latter have since died" (Jarvis 1907: 451). In his short battle report, dated January 26, 1838, Jesup listed two killed and six wounded in the 3d Artillery, one wounded in the 2d Dragoons, and five killed (three of whom were in Captain William J.S. Dearing's company) and 23 wounded among the Tennessee volunteers. Of the wounded, he added "8 dangerously (2 since dead) and 15 slightly" (*NNR*, February 17, 1838: 1:3). In his report to Poinsett the next day, Jesup stated he had a total of seven killed and 31 wounded, including himself in the latter (Procyk 1999: 83). Of Jesup's condition after the battle, an unknown officer of the 3d Artillery reported that he was not "seriously hurt" and was "attending to his duties the same as before" (*VP*, February 28, 1838: 2:4). Fleeing south, the Seminoles left two dead on the battlefield and carried away an unknown number of other casualties as they withdrew further into the swampland.

Of events during the day after the battle, Motte wrote:

> … we remained at our encampment, occupied in taking care of the wounded; preparing litters for their removal; and in the sad offices of interring the dead. Also in ranging the country round about with a portion of the Dragoons; and collecting the horses and cattle left by the enemy in the vicinity, of which we found a great many ponies, and over two hundred head of cattle. The day was also occupied in throwing a bridge over the Locha-Hatchee, and cutting a road through the hammock. [Both of these tasks were accomplished under the skill and supervision of Colonel Gates.] (Sunderman 1953: 197)

Analysis

DADE'S MASSACRE

News of the massacre of the detachment commanded by Dade burst like a thunderclap on the American nation and raised a great clamor for revenge. Yet no one seemed to question how the death of such an experienced US Army officer, and most of those under his command, came to pass. Dade had served in the War of 1812 as a third lieutenant in the 12th Infantry. After transfer to the 4th Infantry in 1815, he led two successful military expeditions along the route from Fort Brooke to Fort King through forbidding wilderness in 1825 and 1826. He commanded the post at Key West, and was eventually assigned to command the southern portion of Florida, running from Cape Florida on the east coast to Charlotte Harbor on the west coast.

Dade's march to Fort King amply demonstrates, however, how a unit could fall victim to an ambush when it neglected proper security measures. On the morning of December 28, 1835, he permitted the detachment marching to the relief of Fort King to proceed without first posting guards on its flanks. Presumably he considered that, as he was more than halfway along the route and had passed through the most dangerous part of the route without being attacked at any of the four river crossings or among the heavy foliage, there was less need to be vigilant. To make matters worse, according to an eyewitness and survivor, shortly before the attack he assured his men that they had "got through all danger" and could look forward to "three days for Christmas" (*BMP*, June 6, 1837: 2:2).

Also, it was remiss of his noncommissioned officers to permit the men under Dade's command to wear their overcoats over their cartridge boxes as protection against the weather on the morning of the attack. This placed them at a distinct disadvantage when required to return fire.

Regarding the gun crew manning the six-pounder gun accompanying the column, they had insufficient time to load and fire due to the suddenness of

the attack, while the close proximity of the Seminoles meant that once the gun crew were ready the solid shot they fired flew over the Seminoles' heads. Meanwhile, the gun crew were rapidly shot down by Seminole sharpshooters.

Furthermore, Dade's African-American scout Louis Pacheco probably served as a Seminole spy and led Dade's relief column into an ambush. How he came into Dade's confidence is a mystery. By 1835, the Seminoles and African Americans had forged a strong alliance that could be traced back at least two generations and of which the US Army had full knowledge. Nevertheless, a breakdown in security had occurred within Dade's command, and Pacheco was allowed to lead 101 men to their deaths.

As for the Seminoles, although there was some hesitation in their ranks because Micanopy wanted to delay action until Osceola and his warriors joined their ranks, the attacks on Dade and Fort King showed the good command and control of Seminole leadership. With warriors trained to fight together, Osceola was able to synchronize these attacks to occur nearly simultaneously.

LAKE OKEECHOBEE

The battle at Lake Okeechobee was counted as a great victory by Taylor because his small army managed to drive back the Seminoles from a strongly held woodland fortress location. In recognition for this he was breveted brigadier general and, on May 15, 1838, succeeded Jesup as commander of all troops in Florida. Taylor's success at Lake Okeechobee was limited, however, because he did not achieve a resounding victory in terms of casualties. In his "Official Report" he stated that his opponents "probably suffered equally

Entitled "Massacre of Major Dade and his Command," this engraving was first published in 1847 in John W. Barber's *Incidents in American History*. It shows Brevet Major General Edmund P. Gaines and his staff officers viewing the site of Dade's Massacre on February 20, 1836. The six-pounder gun stands at right with the fallen soldiers strewn around it, many of whom still clutch their weapons. The advance guard of Gaines' column are shown passing by in the background. Having recovered sufficiently from his wounds, massacre survivor Private Joseph Sprague was by this time attached to the 2d Artillery under Gaines' command, and must have been particularly moved on returning to the battle site. (Internet Archive)

with ourselves" (*NNR*, February 10, 1838: 370:3) but, in fact, his own losses were much greater than those of his enemy with 26 killed and 112 wounded, compared with only ten or 11 Seminoles found dead and 14 wounded on the battlefield. The troops found "traces of blood to the banks of the Okee-cho-bee Lake" (*NNR*, February 10, 1838: 370:3), but even if the Seminoles did carry other dead as well as wounded off the battlefield, US casualties were still a disproportionately high figure for a great victory.

Having a great dislike of volunteer soldiery, Taylor rejected Gentry's suggestion of "a flanking attack to the north or south," rather than a frontal assault, and stated without complete justification in his after-battle report that the Missourians at Lake Okeechobee "mostly broke, and instead of forming in the rear of the regulars, as had been directed … retired across the swamp to their baggage and horses, nor could they be again brought into action as a body" (*NNR*, February 10, 1838: 370:3). Certainly, many of them did run, but others held their ground despite being caught in a murderous crossfire and joined the regulars in pushing forward to drive the Seminoles out of the hammock. In response to Taylor's harsh criticism of the Missourian unit Chiles, who commanded the unit after the death of Gentry, wrote that Taylor's report of his men breaking and running was "utterly unfounded," and that they "mostly not only maintained their ground, but continued to push on" (*JCR*, March 31, 1838: 2:4).

Commenting on the effectiveness of the Seminoles, Taylor further reported on casualties inflicted on the 6th Infantry, stating that the Seminoles succeeded in killing and wounding every officer, as well as most of the non-commissioned officers, including the sergeant major and four of the orderly sergeants (*NNR*, February 10, 1838: 370:3). The performance of the 6th Infantry at Lake

Published in 1847 in John W. Barber's *Incidents in American History,* this engraving depicting the battle of Lake Okeechobee inaccurately shows the advancing US infantry wearing dress uniforms. The Seminoles are more correctly shown firing from the treetops and undergrowth in the hammock. (Internet Archive)

Okeechobee was soon after criticized by Lieutenant Colonel Foster of the 4th Infantry. An advocate of the shock bayonet charge, he wrote his wife that Lieutenant Colonel Thompson had advanced the 6th Infantry too slowly into battle, thereby sustaining heavy casualties (Missall 2005: 126). Yet eventually, as Taylor noted, "the enemy was completely routed, and driven in every direction, and were pursued by the troops until near night, and until they were completely exhausted"; he did concede, though, that "The victory was dearly purchased" (*ANC,* February 1, 1838: 76: 2).

In fact, the Seminoles were not routed and driven in every direction. To withdraw in such a manner was a tactic employed particularly by the Miccosukees and was designed so that they could not easily be tracked to a rendezvous point where the warriors could re-unite to fight another day. As for battle losses, Abiaka and his allies had inflicted the greatest losses on any US force during the Second Seminole War, and one of the heaviest in the annals of Indian warfare on the frontier (Tucker 1991: 165).

THE LOXAHATCHEE RIVER

The last pitched battle of the Second Seminole War, the fight at Loxahatchee River was regarded by US authorities as a decisive victory that persuaded many of the dwindling number of Seminole warriors to turn themselves in for migration west, while others determined to continue the struggle to defend their homeland in much smaller groups. Although the numbers of US troops killed and wounded at the battle were not great, Jesup's frontal attack on a hammock surrounded by swampland – which repeated the tactic used by Taylor at Lake Okeechobee – received some considerable criticism.

During February 1838, an anonymous officer at Fort Pierce, a supply depot on St. Lucie Sound, stated: "Jesup fought across a creek, and after the action discovered that his force was more than sufficient to have surrounded their position, which, from the information I have received, cannot cover more the ten acres of ground" (*DP*, February 13, 1838: 2:3). Later the same month, another officer who appears to have been present at the battle wrote:

> It is the general impression, I believe, that had a proper plan been pursued, every soul of the enemy would have been captured. – We had men enough to have surrounded them and could have done it, but instead, troops, grape-shot, shells, and war-rockets, were all sent pell-mell into the hammock. – The enemy, it is true, were ferited [*sic*] out, but that could have been accomplished without firing a gun. (*VP*, February 23, 1838: 2:4)

Another officer was more positive and recognized the bravery of those under Jesup's command, commenting that "it would have filled your bosom with pleasure to have seen on the day of the battle … these men charge the hammock and swim the creek, in the face of the enemy hid behind their trees, and amidst their fires and savage yells" (*RE*, March 3, 1838: 4:5).

The only known image of Abiaka, war chief of the Miccosukee Seminoles, this sketch was made at Fort Lauderdale by Assistant Surgeon Ellis Hughes in 1839. Abiaka successfully defied the US government and refused to remove to the Indian Territory west of the Mississippi. At the end of the Second Seminole War, a letter published in the *Natchez Weekly Courier*, of Mississippi, dated March 29, 1843, stated that he had proved himself to be "one of the most consummate generals and skilful warriors … he has baffled for the past seven years the most experienced, successful and distinguished of our military commanders … and now roams, free and unmolested, the glorious shore of the Florida Atlantic … To our knowledge, Sam has not been visible to the pale faces since 1837, and nothing definite has been received from him until lately, when at the polite request of Gen. [William J.] Worth for him to 'come in,' he returned the uncourteous [*sic*] answer, 'tustenuggee wahoo bosh,' which literally means when translated, 'I'll see you d____d first.'" (Ellis Hughes Diary, University of South Florida, Cat. No. H38-00001 - Leaf 56 verso)

Aftermath

After the last two battles in south Florida involving large military forces against a dwindling number of Seminoles and their African-American allies, military actions became smaller and involved fewer combatants. Frustrated with the developments of the Indian removal policy, Jesup resigned his position and was replaced by Taylor. Jesup returned to Washington, DC, where he resumed his duties as Quartermaster General of the US Army.

During the next four years, small-scale engagements continued to take place, and increasing numbers of Seminoles were hunted down, often with the use of bloodhounds, and forced to move west to Indian Territory. By 1842 about 4,000 Seminoles had been resettled. The Armed Occupation Act of 1842 encouraged white settlement in the territory, and the Second Seminole War was declared at an end on August 14, 1842. Florida became a state in the Union on March 3, 1845.

The Second Seminole War lasted seven years and probably cost the United States about $30m. No other Native American nation was ever able to hold off the US Army for such a length of time. Of approximately 5,000 Seminoles living in Florida at the beginning of the war, only a few hundred remained at the end of the conflict. There is no record of how many were killed in action. A great many died of disease and starvation during the war, on the trek west, and even after they reached Indian Territory. Regarding the fate of the Black Seminoles, some were sold back into slavery in US plantations, while others were offered their freedom in return for surrender and cooperation with the Army. Many Seminoles felt betrayed and cheated out of their legal property, however, and due to their protestations the Army was unable to fulfill its promise. Hence, many who went west were returned to slavery under the Creek slave codes in Indian Territory. More than 40,000 regular US military personnel, militiamen, and volunteers served in a conflict that cost the lives of about 1,500 regular soldiers, mostly from debilitating tropical disease, plus the lives of an unknown number of volunteers.

Born into slavery, Luis Fatio Pacheco escaped in 1824 but was re-captured and sold several times, eventually becoming the "property" of Antonio Pacheco, a Cuban merchant in Sarasota, Florida. In December 1835, Pacheco was hired as an interpreter by Captain Francis S. Belton, and was detached to accompany Dade's column. Pacheco was one of only three survivors of Dade's Massacre, and was suspected of deliberately leading 101 Americans to their deaths. He eventually achieved freedom and spent much of the remainder of his life attempting to exonerate himself. (Courtesy of Cowan's Auctions)

ORDERS OF BATTLE

Dade's Massacre, December 28, 1835

Seminole forces

Chief Micanopy (Crazy Alligator) plus c.180 Seminole warriors. Casualties: c.3 KIA & 5 WIA = 8.

Dade's column

Total strength: seven officers, one assistant surgeon, one scout/interpreter, one civilian servant, and 98 enlisted men = 108. Total casualties: 105 KIA, 2 WIA, and 1 captured.
HQ: Brevet Major Francis L. Dade commanding, plus six officers, one assistant surgeon, one scout/interpreter, and one civilian servant. Casualties = 9 KIA & 1 captured.
Co. B, 2d Artillery: 9 enlisted men. Casualties: 9 KIA.
Co. C, 2d Artillery: 35 enlisted men. Casualties: 34 KIA & 1 WIA.
Co. H, 2d Artillery: 11 enlisted men. Casualties: 11 KIA.
Co. B, 3d Artillery: 32 enlisted men. Casualties: 31 KIA & 1 WIA but escaped to survive.
Co. B, 4th Infantry: 11 enlisted men. Casualties: 11 KIA.

Lake Okeechobee, December 25, 1837

Seminole forces

Chiefs Abiaka (Sam Jones), Halpatter-Tustenuggee (Alligator), Coacoochee (Wild Cat), plus 400 warriors. Casualties: c.11 KIA & 14 WIA = 25.

US forces

Total strength: c.58 officers plus c.1,295 men. Total casualties: 29 KIA and 111 WIA = 140.
HQ: Colonel Zachary Taylor, 1st Lieutenant J.M. Hill, 2d Infantry, and 1st Lieutenant George H. Griffin, 6th Infantry.
1st Infantry: Lieutenant Colonel William Davenport plus 197 officers and men. Co. A: 1st Lieutenant Joseph H. La Motte; Co. B: Captain Samuel McRee; Co. D: Captain Thomas Barker; Co. E: Captain Albert S. Miller; Co. F: 2d Lieutenant John M. Scott; Co. G: 1st Lieutenant William H. Storer; Co. H: Captain William Day; Co. I: Captain William R. Jouett; Co. K: Captain John J. Abercrombie. Total casualties: 2 WIA (company affiliations not known).
4th Infantry: Lieutenant Colonel William S. Foster and Brevet Major William M. Graham, plus 274 officers and men. Co. A: 1st Lieutenant John L. Hooper (casualties: 1 WIA, 2 KIA); Co. B and Co. C: 1st Lieutenant Richard B. Scriven; Co. D (mounted): 2d Lieutenant William G. Grandin; Co. E: 1st Lieutenant John M. Harvie, 2d Infantry; Co. G and Co. I: 2d Lieutenant and Adjutant Robert C. Buchanan; Co. H: Private Barthol Shumard (casualties: 1 KIA); Co. K (mounted): Captain George W. Allen (casualties: 1 WIA). Total casualties: 3 KIA & 19 WIA = 22 (specific wounded in every company not known).
6th Infantry: Lieutenant Colonel Alexander R. Thompson plus 224 officers and men. HQ: Lieutenant Colonel Alexander R. Thompson, 1st Lieutenant John P. Center (Adjutant); 1st Lieutenant W.H.T. Walker (Adjutant), and Captain George Andrews (Assistant Commissary of Subsistence) (casualties: 2 KIA & 2 WIA); Co. A: 1st Lieutenant Francis J. Brooke, 7th Infantry (casualties: 3 KIA); Co. B: Captain George H. Crossman and 2d Lieutenant Samuel Woods; Co. F: Captain Gustavus Dorr (casualties: 3 KIA & 1 WIA – Dorr himself); Co. G: 1st Lieutenant William Hoffman (casualties: 4 KIA); Co. H: also Captain Gustavus Dorr (casualties: 4 KIA & 1 WIA – Dorr himself); Co. I: Captain Joseph Van Swearingen (casualties: 3 KIA); Co. K: Captain Thomas Noel (casualties: 4 KIA). Total casualties: 23 KIA & 55 WIA (the complete company affiliation of all wounded is not known).
Co. G, 4th Artillery: Captain John Munroe and 35 men.
Missouri Volunteers: Colonel Robert Gentry plus 18 officers and 160 men. Total casualties: 34 (specific KIA and WIA numbers not known).
HQ: Colonel Robert Gentry, Adjutant Hiram G. Parks, Sergeant/Surgeon John A. Hannah, Quartermaster William McDaniel, Commissary A.D. Bradley, Paymaster Thomas Miller, Sergeant Major Richard Gentry, Jr., Quartermaster Sergeant Thomas Bryant, and Principal Musician Elam Herns (casualties: 1 KIA & 1 WIA).
First Battalion: Lieutenant Colonel John W. Price. Co. D: Captain Congreve Jackson and 1st Lieutenant Prior W. Jackson; Co. F: Captain William C. Pollard, 1st Lieutenant Hugh Vanlandingham, and Ensign James McRumsey; Co. G:

Captain James Childs and Ensign Henry Childs. Second Battalion: Major Horatio H. Hughes. Co. K: Captain Thomas D. Grant and 1st Lieutenant Arthanasias Barnet; Co. L: Captain John H. Curd, 1st Lieutenant John Blaky, and Ensign William. H. Winlock; Co. M: Captain Cornelius Gilliam and 1st Lieutenant James Waters; Co. N:

Captain John Sconce, 1st Lieutenant Israel R. Hendley, 2d Lieutenant Patrick Darcy, and Ensign John F. Hughes. **Morgan's Spies:** Lieutenant Colonel Alexander G. Morgan plus 43 men. **Delaware and Shawnee Scouts:** Captain Joseph G. Parks plus 70 men.

The Loxahatchee River, January 24, 1838

Seminole forces
Chiefs Tuskegee and Halleck-Hajo, plus c.300 warriors. Total casualties: 2 confirmed KIA; other casualties not known.

US forces
Major General Thomas S. Jesup plus c.1,500 officers and men. Total casualties: 9 KIA, 30 WIA = 39.
HQ: Major General Thomas S. Jesup, Adjutant 1st Lieutenant Frederick Searle, and Assistant Surgeon Nathan S. Jarvis. Casualties: 1 WIA.
2d Dragoons: Colonel William S. Harney plus c.600 officers and men. Co. A: 2d Lieutenant George A.H. Blake; Co. B: Captain William M. Fulton; Co. C and Co. I: Captain Benjamin L. Beall; Co. D: 2d Lieutenant Nathan Darling; Co. E: 1st Lieutenant Erasmus D. Bullock; Co. F: Captain Townshend Dade; Co. G: Captain William W. Tompkins; Co. H: Captain Henry W. Fowler; Co. K: Captain Edward S. Winder (casualties: 1 WIA). Total casualties: 1 WIA.
3d Artillery: Colonel Lemuel Gates and Major William McClintock, plus c.400 officers and men. Co. A: 2d Lieutenant William Frazer (casualties: 1 KIA); Co. B: 2d Lieutenant

William Mock; Co. C: 1st Lieutenant William Wall (casualties: 1 WIA); Co. D: 1st Lieutenant Robert Anderson (casualties: 2 WIA); Co. E: 2d Lieutenant Jubal A. Early; Co. F: 2d Lieutenant William B. Davidson; Co. G: 2d Lieutenant William T. Sherman; Co. H: 2d Lieutenant Christopher Q. Tompkins (casualties: 1 KIA & 2 WIA); Co. I: 1st Lieutenant Benjamin Poole. Total casualties: 2 KIA & 5 WIA.
4th Artillery: Lieutenant Colonel James Bankhead. Co. B: Captain John M. Washington; Co. D: 1st Lieutenant Edward C. Ross; Co. H: 2d Lieutenant John C. Pemberton.
Tennessee Mounted Infantry Battalion: Major William Lauderdale plus 532 men. Companies led by Captain Darlon A. Wilds and 1st Lieutenant G.B. Gwathney; Captain Benjamin Cherry and 1st Lieutenant William Gipson; Captain Sanders Faris and 1st Lieutenant Isaac Estill; Captain Richard E. Waterhouse and 2d Lieutenant Darius Waterhouse; Captain William L.S. Dearing and 2d Lieutenant Robert Dallis. Total casualties: 7 KIA, 23 WIA. Specific company casualties not known.
North Alabama Volunteers: Lieutenant Colonel David Caulfield, Captain Richard Griffin, plus 100 men.
Delaware Scouts: 35 men.

The Major Dade Monument at the National Cemetery in Augustine, Florida, c.1920. The soldiers were initially buried at the site of the battle, but were re-interred in 1842 under three coquina pyramids at the site. (Courtesy of the State Archives of Florida)

SELECT BIBLIOGRAPHY

Anonymous (1836). *An Authentic Narrative of the Seminole War; and of the Miraculous Escape of Mrs. Mary Godfrey, and her four Female Children.* New York, NY: D.F. Blanchard and Others.

Barr, Captain James (1836). *Correct and Authentic Narrative of the Indian War in Florida with a Description of Maj. Dade's Massacre.* New York City, NY: J. Narine, Printer, 11 Wall Street.

Bell, Christine (2004). "Investigating Second Seminole War Sites in Florida: Identification Through Limited Testing." Unpublished thesis. Tampa, FL: University of South Florida.

Bemrose, John (1966). *Reminiscences of the Second Seminole War 1835–1842.* Gainesville, FL: University of Florida Press.

Brevard, Caroline Mays (1904). *A History of Florida.* New York, NY: American Book Co.

Butler, David S.B. (2001). "An Archaeological Model of Seminole Combat Behavior." M.A. thesis, Department of Applied Anthropology, University of South Florida.

Catlin, George (1845). *Illustrations of the Manners, Customs, and Condition of the North American Indians.* Vol. 2. London: Henry G. Bohn, York Street, Covent Garden.

Coe, Charles H. (1898). *Red Patriot: The Story of the Seminoles.* Cincinnati, OH: The Editor Publishing Co.

Cohen, Myer M. (1836). *Notices of Florida and the Campaigns.* Charleston, SC: Burges & Honour, 18 Broad Street.

Covington, James W. (1993). *The Seminoles of Florida.* Gainesville, FL: University of Florida Press.

Franke, Arthur E. (1977). *Ft. Mellon 1837–42: A Microcosm of the Second Seminole War.* Miami, FL: Banyan Books, Inc.

Gentry, Richard (1909). *The Gentry Family in America 1676–1909.* New York, NY: The Grafton Press.

Gentry, William R. (1918). "The Missouri Soldier One Hundred Years Ago," *Missouri Historical Review* (July), Vol. 12, No. 4: 216–23.

Hamersley, Thomas H.S., ed. (1880). *Complete Army Register of the United States for One Hundred Years (1779–1879).* Washington, DC: T.H.S. Hamersly.

Harvey, Conrad E., Major (2007). "An Army Without Doctrine: The Evolution of US Army Tactics in the Absence of Doctrine, 1779 to 1847." Unpublished thesis. Fort Leavenworth, KS: US Army Command and General Staff College.

Heitman, Francis B. (1903). *Historical Register and Dictionary of the United States Army*, Vol. 1. Washington, DC: Government Printing Office.

Howell, Edgar M. & Donald E. Kloster (1969). *United States Army Headgear to 1854.* Washington, DC: Smithsonian Institution Press.

Hughes, Ellis, papers. Special Collections, University of South Florida Libraries, Tampa, Florida.

Jarvis, N.S. (1907). "An Army Surgeon's Notes of Frontier Service, 1833–48," *Journal of the Military Service Institution of the United States.* Vol. 40 (March–April), No. 146: 269–77.

Kersey Jr., Harry A. & Michael Petersen (1997). "'Was I a Member of Congress …' Zachary Taylor's Letter to John J. Crittenden, January 12, 1838, concerning the Second Seminole War," *Florida Historical Quarterly* (Spring), Vol. 75, No. 4: 447–61.

Mahon, John K., ed. (1960). "The Journal of A.B. Meek and the Second Seminole War, 1836," *Florida Historical Quarterly* (April), Vol. 38, No. 4: 302–18.

Mahon, John K. (2017). *History of the Second Seminole War, 1835–1842.* Gainesville, FL: University of Florida Press.

McCall, George A. (1868). *Letters from the Frontier.* Philadelphia, PA: J.B. Lippincott & Co.

Missall, John & Mary Lou, eds (2005). *This Miserable Pride of a Soldier 1836–1839: The Letters and Journals of Col. William S. Foster in the Second Seminole War.* Tampa, FL: University of Tampa Press.

Monk, J. Floyd (1978). "Christmas Day in Florida, 1837," *Tequesta*, No. 38: 5–38.

Peterkin, Ernest W. (1995). "The United States Army Bootee, 1861–1865," *Military Collector & Historian* (Summer), Vol. XLVII, No. 2: 69–75.

Porter, Kenneth Wiggins (1946). "The Negro Abraham," *Florida Historical Quarterly* (July), Vol. 25, No. 1: 1–43.

Potter, Woodburne (1836). *The War in Florida: Being an Exposition of its Causes and an Accurate History of the Campaigns of Generals, Clinch, Gaines and Scott.* Baltimore, MD: Lewis & Coleman.

Prince, Lieutenant Henry, diary. P.K. Yonge Library of Florida History, University of Florida.

Procyk, Richard J. (1999). *Guns Across the Loxahatchee: Remembering the Seminole Wars.* Cocoa, FL: Florida Historical Society.

Records of the Office of the Quartermaster General (Clothing Bureau), Record Group 92, US National Archives, Washington, DC.

Risch, Erna (1989). *Quartermaster Support of the Army: A History of the Corps, 1775–1939.* Washington, DC: Center of Military History, United States Army.

Rodenbough, Theophilus F. (1875). *From everglade to cañon with the second dragoons.* New York, NY: D. Van Nostrand.

Scott, Major-General Winfield (1825). *Infantry Tactics; or, Rules for the Exercise and Manoeuvres of the Infantry of the U.S. Army.* Washington, DC: Printed by Davis & Force (Franklin's Head), Pennsylvania Avenue.

Scott, Major-General Winfield (1835). *Infantry Tactics in Three Volumes. Infantry-Tactics; or, Rules for the Exercise and Manoeuvres of the United States' Infantry.* New York, NY: George Dearborn.

Smith, William W. (1836). *Sketch of the Seminole War and Sketches During a Campaign.* Charleston, SC: Dan J. Dowling.

Sprague, John T. (1848). *The origin, progress, and conclusion of the Florida war.* New York, NY: D. Appleton & Co.

Sunderman, James F., ed. (1953). *Journey into Wilderness: An Army Surgeon's Account of Life in Camp and Field during the Creek and Seminole Wars 1836–1838 by Jacob Rhett Motte.* Gainesville, FL: University of Florida Press.

Troiani, Don (1998). *Don Troiani's Soldiers in America, 1754–1865.* Mechanicsburg, PA: Stackpole Books.

Tucker, Phillip Thomas (1991). "A Forgotten Sacrifice: Richard Gentry, Missouri Volunteers, and the Battle of Okeechobee," *Florida Historical Quarterly* (October), Vol. 70, No. 2: 150–65.

US Congress (1834). *American State Papers.* Documents, Legislative and Executive, of the Congress of the United States. "Indian Affairs," Vol. 2. Washington, DC: Gales & Seaton.

US Congress (1836). *An authentic narrative of the Seminole War.* Providence, RI: Printed for D.F. Blanchard.

US Congress (1860). *American State Papers* "Military Affairs," Vol. 5. Washington, DC: Gales & Seaton.

US Congress (1861). *American State Papers* "Military Affairs," Vol. 7. Washington, DC: Gales & Seaton.

US Treasury Department (1840). *Receipts and Expenditures of the United States for the Year 1839.* Washington, DC: Blair & Rives.

US War Department (1834). *General Regulations for the Army.* Washington, DC: Printed by Francis P. Blair.

Walkiewicz, Kathryn (2008). "Portraits and Politics: The Specter of Osceola in *Leaves of Grass*," *Walt Whitman Quarterly Review* (Winter), Vol. 25: 108–15.

West, Patsy (2016). "Abiaka, or Sam Jones, in Context: The Mikasuki Ethnogenesis through the Third Seminole War," *Florida Historical Quarterly* (Winter), Vol. 94, No. 3: 3–115.

West, Samuel & William S. Belko, eds (2011). *Seminole Strategy, 1812–1858: A Prospectus for Further Research.* Gainesville, FL: University Press of Florida.

White, Frank F. & Robert C. Buchanan (1950). "A Journal of Lt. Robert C. Buchanan during the Seminole War," *Florida Historical Quarterly*, Vol. 29, No. 2: 132–51.

White, Nathan W. (1981). *Private Joseph Sprague of Vermont, the last soldier-survivor of Dade's Massacre in Florida, 28 December, 1835.* Fort Lauderdale, FL: N.W. White.

Newspapers and other local publications

Army and Navy Chronicle, Washington, DC (*ANC*); *Boston Morning Post*, Boston, MA (*BMP*); *Cahawba Democrat*, Cahawba, AL (*CD*); *Charleston Courier*, Charleston, SC (*CC*); *The Charleston Daily Courier*, Charleston, SC (*CDC*); *Charleston Mercury*, Charleston, SC (*CM*); *Commercial Journal*, Austin, TX (*CJ*); *Daily Picuyune*, New Orleans, LA (*DP*); *Jefferson City Republican*, Jefferson City, MO (*JCR*); *Missouri Argus*, St. Louis, MO (*MA*); *National Gazette*, Philadelphia, PA (*NG*); *Newbern Spectator*, Newbern, NC (*NS*); *Niles' National Register*, Washington, DC (*NNR*); *Richmond Enquirer*, Richmond, VA (*RE*); *Vermont Phœnix*, Brattleboro, VT (*VP*); *The Weekly Standard*, Raleigh, NC (*WS*).

INDEX